BY TAYL

BALLGAMES TO BOARDROOMS

Leadership, Business and Life Lessons

From Our Coaches We Never Knew We Needed

Quantity sales special discounts are available on quantity purchases by corporations, associations, and others. For details, contact the publisher at the address above.

Orders by U.S. trade bookstores and wholesalers. Email info@BeyondPublishing.net

The Beyond Publishing Speakers Bureau can bring authors to your live event. For more information or to book an event contact the Beyond Publishing Speakers Bureau speak@BeyondPublishing.net

The Author can be reached directly at **www.BallgamesToBoardrooms.com** and **BeyondPublishing.net/AuthorSpeakerTaylorScott**

Book Cover Design: Kevin Vain, CoLab Creative Group
Ballgames To Boardrooms logo design: Steve Barkofski
Manufactured and printed in the United States of America distributed globally by BeyondPublishing.net

BEYOND
PUBLISHING

New York | Los Angeles | London | Sydney
Library of Congress Control Number: 2017946533

10 9 8 7 6 5 4 3 2 1   978-1-947256-92-7
First Beyond Publishing soft cover English edition August 2017 $12.97 USA $18.97 Canada
First Beyond Publishing hard cover English edition August 2017 $17.97 USA $24.97 Canada

BUSINESS & ECONOMICS / Hospitality, Travel & Tourism, Mentoring & Coaching SELF-HELP / Communication & Social Skills

"Taylor Scott has brilliantly packaged a way forward for Millennials and leaders of Millennials to not only coexist in Corporate America, but to also transform menial jobs into meaningful work. If you loved playing sports as a kid or even as an adult, but find yourself stuck in a career hamster wheel, this book is for you. Prepare to reignite the child-like faith you had back then, realizing actionable steps toward new realms of happiness and success today." - **Eric Chester - Bestselling Author of *On Fire At Work: How Great Companies Ignite Passion in Their People Without Burning Them Out*, Award Winning Keynote Speaker, and the Founder of the Center for Work Ethic Development.**

"Read this book for new ideas to make you a better leader." - **Mark Sanborn – President, Sanborn & Associates Inc. Bestselling Author of *The Fred Factor* and *You Don't Need a Title to be a Leader***

"Picking up *Ballgames to Boardrooms* is entering into a personal conversation with Taylor. He connects sports to real life, focusing on the corporate setting as a big part of life. The well-reasoned and well-articulated advice provides the sort of coaching we all need to be the sort of team player, coach, partner, friend, and person we sometimes lose sight of who we want to strive to be. Practical advice, and applicable wisdom, providing a guide to self-reflection to help you build on your own potential. A book worth reading, and advice worth taking..." – **Dr. Michael Sturman, *The Kenneth and Marjorie Blanchard Professor of Human Resources* – Cornell University**

"Taylor Scott has blended faith, sports, entertaining stories, and uncommon wisdom to create a book that not only points the way for you to be more successful in life, you will become a better, happier, and more fulfilled person in the process." – **Mark Youngblood, CEO of Inner Mastery, Inc. and author of Dear Human, Master Your Emotions**

"*Ballgames to Boardrooms* is a playbook for true professionals. It encourages readers to find their passion, believe in it, and never lose sight of the bigger picture." – **Jennifer Ridgley, Sr. Director of Communications – Pittsburgh Penguins**

FOREWORD

BY MARK SANBORN

Coaches impact us, for better or for worse.

When I was young I played little league baseball. I was an overweight kid with the hand eye coordination of a turnip. No surprise, but I did not excel. You know what I remember about my coach? Not much. He didn't teach me anything that stuck, nor exemplify the kind of person I wanted to be. And I don't remember him ever encouraging me. I don't even remember his name.

But what about the coaches with real positive impact? The ones who change you forever in positive ways with their advice, encouragement and example?

Taylor Scott has written a book about how to learn from great coaches. And in the process he becomes your improvement coach.

Taylor has accumulated experience and wisdom beyond his years.

I met him through my book, The Fred Factor. He's been a fan and advocate of that book and used to write a blog about the "Freds" he met.

If you're not familiar, the book is about a postal carrier who was able to turn the ordinary into the extraordinary. And after all, we all have ordinary moments, but choose what to do with them. The big point of the book is that nobody can prevent you from choosing to be extraordinary. And it was obvious to me that Taylor—like Fred—was committed to turning ordinary into extraordinary in his life and career.

Taylor did some training around The Fred Factor on behalf of my company. His years at developing his public speaking paid off, and he delivered great presentations around the themes in the book.

When he worked with us, he was obviously a man on a mission. I knew he was destined to do great things. He's a committed learner and a person who believes in having lots of experiences to learn from.

I had the opportunity to visit him in Las Vegas and met his parents while they were visiting there too. That gave me an insight into why Taylor was such a good guy. He comes from a good family that taught him well.

I appreciate him because he is a person of faith, and not afraid to share his beliefs in a time when many are hesitant to take a stand.

Taylor has done a lot of moving around, in the process always moving upward. He has the ability to apply what he learned yesterday into whatever he is doing today.

So now you are holding another output of Taylor's prodigious efforts. Through stories and observations, you won't just be reading what Taylor did and learned. You'll be benefiting from what you can learn to make your life and business better.

We all need a coach in our journey, someone we can learn from, and someone who can inspire us. Taylor is that kind of person and he has written this book to guide you on your journey in turning the ordinary into the extraordinary.

Enjoy!

Mark Sanborn
President, Sanborn & Associates

For Nora Jane and Henry, my niece and nephew.

And for every up and comer on the verge of a career breakthrough, but currently feeling stuck…

I wrote this for you.

Meaningful work, hope, encouragement, fulfillment, and happiness are closer than you think…

INTRODUCTION

I didn't invent the concept of going the extra mile. I don't even put it into practice 100 percent of the time. Like you, I'm human. However, I'm passionate about it and I gave it a new title. I call it going OneMoreStep.

In 2005 in my mid-twenties, I worked in Sales for Walt Disney Parks and Resorts, living in Orlando, FL. Four years earlier, I'd just graduated from Florida Southern College. So there I was, about four years into the corporate grind when I realized the simple concept of going OneMoreStep could completely change the game for anyone at any time.

One day in the midst of the corporate chaos I found myself in my "officle" needing to partner with a colleague who was on the other side of the building. It was something relatively important, however, not necessarily earth shattering. I simply needed to send something to her, ultimately making sure we were aligned before sending it back to a client. At Disney, everything is a team effort. Or at least that's the goal.

Sitting at my computer, I first started to send her an email. Then, I thought about it. "That feels like a short cut; and it may take a few days to get a response. Or worse, the purpose of my note may be lost in translation over email," I said to myself. So, I thought, "Maybe I'll give her a call. Hmmmm. Nah. She's just on the other side of the building, maybe I'll actually walk over and speak with her in person."

So, I did. I grabbed what I needed, a few documents in a folder, a pen, and my notebook, and it dawned on me, this all started with an email I was going to write. Instead I took the next step and thought about making a phone call. Finally, I decided to go one more step, and physically walk over to my colleague's office.

On my walk over, as I took step after step, it was like a scene in a movie playing out in my head. I thought how much more efficient an in-person conversation would be, the clarity and brevity both my colleague and I would enjoy. I thought about the time it would save both of us and our client, and how everyone would be able to check this "thing" off our list once and for all, in short order; just because I took **OneMoreStep.**

It may sound trivial, but that's kind of the point. None of it was hard, nor did it take extreme effort or cost a million dollars. All it took was a little extra, just one more step than I thought I'd take at first. Since then, I've been fascinated with how much magic we can create by simply going *one more step.*

Five years later, after leaving my role at Disney, completing my graduate studies at Cornell University and while working in Las Vegas, I started blogging about the topic. The title of the blog was OneMoreStepRevolution, and its purpose was to inspire a revolution encouraging people to break out of their rut by taking the focus off themselves and focus on making magic for others instead.

I shared amazing real life stories about people with whom I worked. Some posts were about family and friends. Others were about simple thoughts, concepts, or topics related to the idea of going OneMoreStep for people. Sometimes it's the literal one more step; other times it's the mental OneMoreStep that makes a difference that matters for people and ultimately for ourselves.

The more I blogged the more I connected with people from all over America. The more I heard from people across all walks of life, industries, and age groups, I realized most of us are out here battling through the peaks and valleys of life, running into the same situations, opportunities, triumphs, and failures. Whether it's the corporate world or just "the world" in general, life gets tedious for everybody.

My passion is helping people feel better about themselves and their current situations at work and at home. I've set out to share hope and encouragement for people who find themselves stuck. That's pretty much everyone, at one point or another.

Re-igniting the Spark

Today's frontline employees, entry-level managers, middle managers, and even some executives, are caught in the proverbial *hamster-in-a-wheel* routine that is Corporate America. A general lack of inspiration and motivation looms over people who spend their days, trudging through life as *real world "Eeyores."* This happens for many reasons spanning issues including poor leadership to bad attitudes not to mention insecurity and a sense of fear. You may be experiencing fear of failure, fear of loss whether it's about losing money, status, or the same job that causes so much pain and anguish in the first place.

Does this sound familiar? Me too. I'm no different from you. I've spent the past 15 years

- Getting frustrated with the slackers
- Bosses who "boss around" as opposed to connecting and leading,
- The "unfair system," and
- The tediousness of the grind

Too often we spend hours, which turn into days and weeks, which turn into months and years wasting time. We may feel mentally paralyzed and as if all hope is lost. I see it and feel it around me and have for many years.

- Do you feel you'll "never be promoted at work" and "someone else will always have what you want?"
- Have you literally lost that loving feeling for what you once thought would be the right professional or personal path, for you?
- Do you constantly want to win, but always feel defeated?

First, I want to let you know, it's okay. It's okay to not be okay. But you don't have to stay there. You can re-ignite the spark you used to have inside. My guess is for all the reasons above; you've picked up this book. I'm glad you did, because in the upcoming pages you and I will engage and connect over stories, illustrations, easy-to-follow action steps and perhaps some fresh perspective that may help.

Remember when we were little? Remember playing sports? We were so innocent, with child-like faith. We just wanted to go play. Our parents dropped us off at practice or the games and all that mattered was having fun, making new friends, learning, growing, and hopefully winning. We had the spark during every game, every practice.

- If you're looking for ways to have more fun at work and home, make new friends or foster more productive professional or personal relationships, keep reading.
- Or, if you're looking for inspiration to reignite your fire to learn, grow or maybe even get that promotion or new job, yes, you picked up the right book.

Soon you'll meet my High School Basketball Coach, Charles Baker. He always taught us to focus on three things – Play Hard, Have Fun, and Listen to Your Coaches. In the chapters that follow, I'll highlight what many of us have forgotten from those simple, yet profound lessons we learned playing sports at a younger age.

Our Little League baseball, basketball, soccer, cheerleading, gymnastics, dance, and football coaches taught us the ideal values and dropped *pearl after pearl* of wisdom we never knew we needed back then. But if we apply those lessons today, at work, we'll see and feel real, positive change. I'm bringing these pearls of wisdom back, which I hope inspires and encourages anyone and everyone who wants a *change* in their day-to-day grind. Hope is alive and well. It's out there. There's a way to experience better days, at home and at work.

I've been leading Teams in the Hospitality and Travel Industry for 15 years, and like you, I've loved sports my whole life. My academic experiences include East Carter High School in Grayson, KY, Florida Southern College, in Lakeland, FL for my Bachelor's Degree, and Cornell University's School of Hotel Administration for a Master's Degree in the Management of Hospitality.

I'm also a devout Christian with many stories of how God has and continues to show up in my life as well as in the lives of others – at work and at home. I know people need encouragement because I'm one of them.

I've been blessed thus far in my professional career; having worked in many different roles including front line and leadership positions, for companies like Disney Parks & Resorts, Gaylord Hotels & Resorts, Starwood Hotels & Resorts, Wynn & Encore Las Vegas, The Cosmopolitan of Las Vegas, and Disney Vacation Club.

I've realized what brings me joy, inspiration and fulfillment. While I love basketball, that's not it. While I love hotels and all facets of the hospitality industry, that's not it, either.

I love helping people. I love helping you.

So, I didn't write this book to get rich. I didn't do it for fame or fortune. I wrote this book to connect with people, and to reconnect them back to what makes them happy; having fun, being utilized for their special talents, winning, and growing; both personally and professionally.

I took Coach Baker's three main lessons: Play Hard, Have Fun, and Listen to Your Coaches. To that I've added two more principles, Practice the Future Today and Make the Extra Pass (Unleash Compassion), which will help you have more fun, feel more fulfilled, and grow in your personal life as well as your professional career.

I hope you're as excited as I am. Better days are closer than you think.

Tip off…

PART ONE

PRACTICE THE FUTURE TODAY

PRACTICE

CHAPTER 1

Growing up, my high school basketball coaches would tell us, *"GS...GS...GS..."* That stood for, "**Game Shots**, from **Game Spots, for Game Situations.**"

It meant before, during, and/or after ***practice*** when shooting around while warming up or working on our game, we should *practice* "game shots" in realistic "game spots" and prepare for real life "game situations." Compare that to wasting time clowning around with NBA-esque lay-up lines, shots from half court, or crazy whirling dervish shots we'd probably never do in a real game situation. It was about capitalizing on every second of our time on the court practicing.

Sometimes life doesn't give us quite what we had in mind. Are you there right now? If you're like me, some of this sounds familiar. You've dreamed about this moment, this job, or this opportunity for a long time. Now that it's happening and you're in "the" job you thought you wanted, you find yourself tasked with doing random things for random reasons and for random people. Or, maybe you're not quite in the job you *think* you should have. Perhaps you're not living in the city you *think* you should be.

Do you often wonder if your role, contributions, or efforts are valued or even appreciated? Do you see your friends or former classmates making all this money, in their corner offices, with their expense accounts, living in their posh condo or suburban home with a white picket fence, and wonder if you'll ever get there? If you're like me, you may often think, "Really? I have to do all of this while *they* get all that? This is what it's come down to?"

Think of "Today" as *Practice*.

Regardless of the situation or scenario, we can always, always, always find ways to practice today for the future God has in store for us. It's a simple idea: your "today job" doesn't have to be your "forever job."

When we embrace every single day and every situation as *practice* for the future, we start thinking about things differently. Suddenly we begin finding solutions rather than dwell on problems. We become ambassadors of PMA (positive mental attitude) in our communities, teams, families, and organizations. We worry less and focus more. We find ourselves driving more business, executing initiatives, and truly adding value to people around us. The notion that you're *practicing* for the future can have an impact on your "today." It makes today relevant, no matter how annoying or frustrating your "today situation" is now.

Every opportunity around every corner in our day-to-day routines, no matter how big or small, can be a chance to *practice*; but it's up to you. When you focus on capitalizing on every opportunity to *practice*, you learn new things, further develop your abilities, and master your skills. Our future self will thank us for having *practiced* along the way.

So, when you feel frustrated or down, and the easy thing to do is to just give up, mail it in, and throw in the "mental towel," go OneMoreStep mentally. *Practice* something. Chances are, no matter what the situation, we can all find something to *practice*, today, so our "future selves" are better off.

Annoyed Today – Expert Tomorrow

If you're not in the role you know you could or should have, so what? Who says you can't grow into it? Remember, this is just a season. We're not defined by our past or even our current performances. Focus less on your past performance; zero in on your potential.

What about you? Are you doing what you've always dreamed you'd do? If so, great! Now's the time to embrace this season of your life, and further hone and sharpen your sword. However, if you currently find yourself in one industry or job but would rather be in a different one, take advantage of the time to practice your future today.

For example, if you are currently in Sales but would rather be in an Operations role, no problem. Volunteer to champion specific projects or initiatives that'll aid in your development for an "operations focused" role in the future. If you're currently in health care but would rather be in finance, ask for ways to work with numbers today, so when a finance job opens up, you'll be ready. If you're currently a teacher or an administrator but you would rather be in Sales, hakuna matata. Actively seek out ways you can *practice* persuading, influencing and counseling fellow educators, administrators, or even students. This is a great way to *practice* your ability to show the value of a product or service, in a sales role down the road.

Right about now, some readers may be wondering, "Hey! What about me? I still don't know what I want to be when I grow up! I don't know what I want to do next. What do I practice today if I'm feeling clueless about what I want tomorrow?"

Great question.

First, relax, take a deep breath, and know you're not alone. Many people of all ages and in all walks of life ask themselves the same question. You're just brave enough to admit you don't really know what you want to do. That's okay. It's okay to not be okay. It's okay to be unsure of exactly what you "want to be when you grow up" or what kind of job you'd like next.

Visualize Who You Want to Be

If you're unsure what you want to do next, you can always practice being a great person. This whole game of life doesn't have to be all about "status" or what job you have anyway. Take the pressure off yourself, and focus on who you're becoming as opposed to what job you'll do next. Become the person your dream boss is looking for and you just might find yourself in the position you always wanted sooner versus later. More on what's really attractive to current and prospective bosses in Chapter 5.

Whether you practice for the type of work you'd rather be doing or practice being the person you know you could or should be in the future, remember to visualize your desired outcome every day. Just like golfers, on the driving range or practice greens, visualize your "shot in life" as you're taking practice swings.

For years, I've worked out with fitness trainers, and they always say, "Visualize the reps." They say it so I'll focus and concentrate on building and strengthening the muscles they know I want keep in shape. By visualizing your desired outcomes, you can do a better job staying focused, doing what it takes to achieve them.

It's true what coaches say about practice. How you practice is how you'll play the game.

Whatever your current situation, if you're in that awkward, mental and emotional downward spiral, and feel like you're losing control of everything, take a 20-second time out. Look around and think about where you'd rather be. Talk to God about it and start *practicing*. With

"The Bellagio was practice..."

~ Steve Wynn

His help, you'll not only make it back on your path toward your goals, but you'll also feel better about life, your current job, and yourself along the way.

YOUR VISION, HIS VISION, AND WHAT NOT TO DO

CHAPTER 2

Andy Stanley's book, Visioneering, is as inspiring as it is eye opening. Andy teaches us God has a vision for every one of us. That includes you and me. He even knows the number of hairs on our heads. One of my favorite verses, Jeremiah 29:11, assures us God not only loves us, He also has "plans" for us. God's plan is way bigger than your current situation. He knows our potential, because He, well, He created us. So, we can be fairly sure He knows. When I read Andy's book, it was God's way of telling me it's time. I heard it and felt it, loud and clear. Time for me to write this book that's been on my heart and mind for years.

Visualize and Reverse Engineer

In my OneMoreStep Revolution blog I expanded on the idea that when we think we've done enough, going OneMoreStep mentally, physically, literally or figuratively, makes magic for others and opens the door to the magic of what I call The OneMoreStep Revolution to unfold for you and everyone around you.

I wrote and published a post about once a week or every two weeks. If I felt the magic, sometimes even twice a week. I was as passionate about the topics of Leadership, Teamwork, Service and Love then as I am today. I knew I liked writing, inspiring, teaching, and coaching, and I knew someday I wanted to write a book.

I started the blog back when I wasn't thrilled about where I was. I didn't want to live in Las Vegas or work in casinos anymore so it gave me a chance to practice the future. I was practicing for a potential opportunity to be an author, speaker, consultant, or maybe even a personal coach someday. Many of my posts from several years ago, provided the foundation for the chapters you'll read in this book.

Visualize where you want to be and what you want to do. Then, reverse engineer backwards. Start by:

- Reverse engineering and mastering the skills you need
- Seek out and gain the knowledge you need to gain.
- Foster the relationships you need to foster to
- Grow into where and who you want to be. So, you
- Practice the future you want to create today

What Not to Do

I'd just accepted a job in Las Vegas, a city I'd given a shot 18-months prior only to find out I either wasn't ready or I didn't like living there. I didn't enjoy the atmosphere, working in casinos. I left Las Vegas after a short stint, pursuing another line of work for a different company within the Hospitality industry in South Florida. I ended up losing my job. A few months later I found myself back in Las Vegas again, the only place where I could find work in 2010.

Honestly, I returned to Las Vegas kicking and screaming. I didn't think it was where I should live and work. I thought I'd hate it just like the first time around. I was so nervous I could barely see straight. Plus, things weren't working out quite as I'd planned. Note: "...quite like I'd planned…" (Count the number of times I used "I" in that paragraph – insert self-eye-roll emoji here.)

My plan was to leave Disney, go to graduate school, get a job in Vegas, rise a few rungs up the corporate ladder, then return to Disney as an awesome, super-conscientious-friendly, super smart-charismatic Disney executive (*Early in my career I had a business crush on every single Disney executive*).

Everything was working out just as I planned until the part where I, well let's see, until the part where I lost "the girl," and I lost my job twice. Both were incredible opportunities God put in my lap. However, I had the audacity to scoff and turn up my nose at them because they didn't align with "my plan." Then, I was turned down on the next 75 to 100 job applications to positions I thought did "align with my plan." I spiraled out of control mentally and emotionally and ended up losing control of everything. I wallowed in my own self-pity for reasons I'm embarrassed to share with you today.

Um. So. Yeah. That happened.

A Fast Pass Through Adversity

Here are a few things I'd like to pass along. Not because I'm better than you, because I'm not. Not because I'm talking down to you or because I think less of you. I certainly don't. But because I've been there. I messed up, wasting several precious years of my twenties. I lost friends, relationships, jobs, and missed out on opportunities to enjoy and rest in God's blessings and plans He specifically designed for me.

I don't want you to do the same. So, this is my attempt to give you a fast pass through adversity. I'm also including a few quick answers to save you from a tough life test, or, pull you out of a mental and emotional downward spiral like I experienced:

- First, start by knowing that God has a plan for you.
- Let Him be in control, because the more you try to be in control, and the tighter you grip the wheel, the further and quicker you spiral out of control.
- It's okay to not be okay, but you don't have to stay that way.

You're no match for this world, this one situation, one annoying job or seemingly rough, tough, unfair world. None of us mere mortals are a match, but God's love and vision for us is awesome. As in, it's awe-inspiring and truly awe-some because He and His plans have, can, and will do things we simply cannot. I've tried. You've tried. How did that work out for us?

Maybe things were okay for a while, but we simply can't do it alone, long term. By ourselves, we can't sustain all "the stuff" the world throws at us. But love can. God's love can do anything, anytime. More on this in Chapter 26.

Trust the Good Lord as Your Captain

So, believe in yourself, for sure. Lean into the vision you have for yourself. Give yourself a break and take some pressure off. Realize you don't have to be The Captain of Your Vision Ship. It's your vision, yes. Just remember God has one for you, too. If your vision clashes with God's vision, that's okay. It's healthy and probably divine. At that point, trust in Him and trust He may know a thing or two about you, which perhaps you don't realize just yet. It could be He's put you in a specific spot among specific people for a specific reason; *perhaps a chance to practice your future today.*

This can be hard to see and feel in moments of stress, distress, and despair. *When you feel God's absence, trust His presence.* It's real, and it's amazing. Just trust it. Trust Him. Garth Brooks said it well in one of his best songs of all time, The River:

"I know I'll hit rough waters, and I know I'll take some falls, but with the good Lord as my captain, I can make it through them all!"

My point to all this and the bow I'll tie on this story during one of the most trying "seasons of my life" so far is when we trust that God has a plan, we realize the pressure we've experienced is simply pressure we put on ourselves.

When I was *practicing* writing my blog all those years ago, and *practicing* my public speaking, my frustrations dissipated, and my *annoyed-o-meter* went to zero. My fulfillment and engagement skyrocketed. I was helping people, coaching people, and consulting people; not to mention learning from those exact same people. I was *practicing* and God was using that time (*waiting time is not always wasted time*) to prepare me for this moment, right now, in this place. He wanted me to share with you some ideas that may help you, inspire you, or touch you at a time when you need it. Not a coincidence, it was His plan all along. He's working in your life now. He's always preparing you for something down the road. Crazy, but isn't it awesome?

By the way, that "awful town" of Las Vegas? The place I thought I didn't want to live? And that industry of gaming and casino resorts that didn't "align with my plan?" Yeah, that one. It changed me for the better. God changed me for good, ala "Wicked" when Ga-Linda was *changed for good* through her journey with Elphie. To this day, I now love Las Vegas. I love the people with whom I worked for so many years in that town. I will forever be grateful God planted me in Las Vegas for four years.

He knew what He was doing. It turned out His plan was better than I ever imagined my plan could or would be. I could be wrong, but I'm sure those years and seasons in Las Vegas were to prepare me for a future only God knew then and still knows today. All you and I must do is trust He has your plan mapped out and it's a good one. Those years may have been to transform my thoughts, goals, and aspirations to shift from being obsessed with working for and improving the Magic Kingdom (Disney) to furthering God's Kingdom.

As you turn the page to Chapter 3 we'll start diving into the strategies it takes to go OneMoreStep, starting from where you find yourself right now to go where you want to be. The focus in Chapter 3 is illustrating how representing your nation well can make a huge difference to you and everyone in your world. You may not have considered that your representation of yourself impacts how you're perceived and, as a result, can set you up for success and a better life.

We've only just met, but if you were to stop reading this book now, and I hope you don't, I want you to at least remember this much from our time together: Visualize what you want, but be open to receive God's vision and plan for you. Trust He has a plan, and believe it's a good one. He promised and he keeps His promises. He's God. He's cool like that.

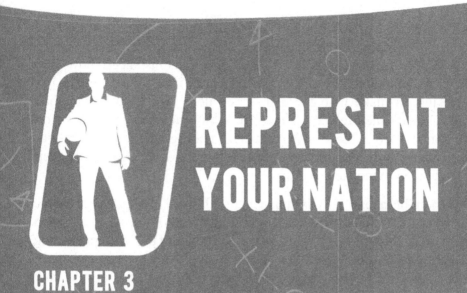

REPRESENT YOUR NATION

CHAPTER 3

I love the Olympics.

I was eight years old when I fell in love with the essence and spirit of the Summer Olympics. I remember watching the Seoul games at every opportunity. I leaned in when the commentators would share the back-stories of some of the athletes and inspiring video interludes to "the Games of the XXIV Olympiad."

I loved it then and I'm still crazy about the Games now.

Inspiration from Sports

I'm fascinated with sports for countless reasons. My favorite thing about sports is the inspiration it provides as participants and fans. I recall broadcaster Bob Costas delivering a great introduction to a prime time telecast of the 2012 Summer Olympics in London. His words are often inspiring during his monologues, leading into or ending each telecast. However, his narrative that evening struck a particularly emotional chord.

Bob Costas began his monologue as the lead-in music faded. "They compete to win, but often they represent so much more…" He went on to tell more stories about a few athletes' circumstances, how they overcame incredible obstacles and the hurdles they managed to rise above just to make it to the games, let alone win a medal for their country and themselves. The broadcast included a few short testimonials, from those same athletes. During this time, each one talked about how important and rewarding it was to represent their nation at the Olympics.

I thought about it. Olympians are ultimate competitors. While individual achievement and accolades may drive them, a common thread runs through each and every Olympian. They're representing their nation. Win or lose, often in interviews with the media before, during, and after their magical Olympic moment, they always talk about what an amazing opportunity it is to represent their country. The way they carry out and follow through on "representing their nation" is forever their own personal brand or stamp regardless of where they end up, be it on or off the podium of winners. It often sets them apart and sets them up for their "next thing in life" whether it's a product endorsement, a spot on the speaking circuit, a job as a sports broadcaster, or even a place on their country's next Olympic team.

We All Belong to a Nation, Represent it Well

What a profound principle for all of us in our careers. You and I aren't Olympians, but we all come from somewhere. Or, we currently belong to a subgroup of the population with whom we share many things in common.

na•tion /ˈnāSHən/
Noun:
1. A large aggregate of people united by common descent, history, culture, or language, inhabiting a particular country or territory.

We all belong to a "nation" of some sort. In some way, shape, or form, we're all part of something bigger than ourselves. Think about who and what you're a part of in your life or career.

What or whom do you "represent?"

Whether it's your family, your hometown, your home state, your home country, your school, or even your company; you belong. Even within your own company, chances are you belong to a particular department or team.

Whatever "aggregate of people" to which you belong, it makes sense to always represent your nation well.

If you're not exactly bounding out of bed each morning like Tigger, happily hopping out the door to get to work, but instead you drag yourself like Eeyore with a cloud following you around all day; consider who and what you represent. Better yet, think about how well you're representing them, your nation, whomever that is for you.

How you carry yourself today, even when times are difficult, will either make your nation proud or let them down. The older you become the more life experiences you've had, for better or worse. The more experiences you have, the more people you meet and the more likely it is you "belong" to a certain group, or "nation."

Networking and reputation, while not the end all be all, go a long way in our constant pursuit of creating a better life. You may wonder will I make the right impression and be well received? What about your family? The reputation and "street credibility" of your school, hometown, state, country, company, or even the team to which you belong at work depends on you. Don't you owe it to yourself and the nations to which you belong, to represent yourself as well as you possibly can? Of course you do.

Take pride in who you are. Take pride in your town or city, state, schools and country from which you've come. While you're at it, take pride in being a part of your team at the company where you work. What if everyone did that? What if everyone took it upon him or herself to straight up represent their nations, teams, departments, and hometowns well? I don't know about you, but that's a world I want to be a part of creating. It starts with us, individuals, like you and me.

Wherever you are today, wherever you're from, and to whichever nation you belong, represent it well. Go OneMoreStep, if for no other reason than to simply represent your nation. You never know how it could help someone else from your own hometown, school, company or your department. When you "represent your nation well" it'll inspire others to follow your lead and represent it well, too. That's not only good for everyone involved; it's also a way to manufacture a sense of purpose in an otherwise dreadful job or situation. Think twice about sending that edgy email, or maybe even pause and consider what to say and how to say it. You may just represent your nation so you get the nod for a promotion you otherwise wouldn't have received. Representing your own team well can only mean good things for the team's credibility. If the team wins, you win. The only variable is the time it takes for those "wins" to accumulate and transform into a better opportunity in the future.

You might be wondering, "Okay, great. Sounds like a novel concept. But how exactly do I "represent my nation well?"

Simple. No, really. Just do all the simple stuff you've probably heard before such as:

- Dress appropriately, which means dress for the job you want, not the one you currently hold.
- Develop a firm handshake. No limp handshakes, be firm but don't crush.
- Make eye contact, and smile at people. Do it often.
- Speak clearly, with emphasis and enthusiasm on what matters. Never mumble.
- Walk, sit, and stand with great posture. Not everyone does, and when you walk tall and with purpose, people notice the difference.
- Be slow to speak, quick to listen, and very slow to anger. If this sounds familiar, it's from James 1:19. I still haven't mastered it 100 percent of the time. Occasionally, I still beat myself up. It would behoove me to follow that powerful concept all the time.
- Exude professionalism and professional maturity. Handle every email, conversation, and situation with style, grace, and kindness. With 100 percent certainty, everyone falls short on this, so it'll set you apart.

I could go on, but you get the point. Most of these ideas are common, simple ones. However common sense can be uncommon. So, they can be tough to pull off, especially in tense, heated moments. You can bet, however you, your team, your department, and your company will be well-represented if you're seen as a person who always embodies these traits. Don't forget "representing" when it comes to your family, your hometown, your school, and maybe even your generation of peers.

It's Our Job, and That's Enough

Mac MacAnally, a Grammy award-winning singer/songwriter wrote a song recorded by one of my favorite artists, Jimmy Buffett, entitled, "It's My Job." Buffett recorded a live album several years ago. He had Mac introduce the song before performing it, beautifully as always.

I love Mac's set up of the song. In his introduction he says, "…Well, it's a song about takin' pride in what ya do for a livin' which I think is a fairly important thing. 'Cause even if you have a job that sucks, it's the quickest way to a job that sucks less. That's my theory, anyway…"

The lyrics of course tell a few stories illustrating the concept of, "It's my job." One illustration is of a street sweeper who's just sweepin' away, whistling as he goes, bouncing with every step. When another man asks why he swept, the street sweeper simply replies:

"It's my job, it's my job to be cleaning up this mess, and that's enough reason to go for me. It's my job to be better than the rest, and that makes the day for me."

Buffett sings the powerful lyrics with heart. The man who asked the question thinks to himself, *"If street sweepers can smile, then I've got no right to be upset…"*

I tear up, with a lump in my throat, every time I hear that song or when I sing it. I just nailed, by the way, singing out loud as I write. I love the sentiment because it reminds me how hard people work. In fact, the people who work hardest always seem to get the least amount of praise, recognition, or glory; yet they keep giving 110 percent all the same. That always inspires me to do things well, whatever the "thing of the moment" may be. It could be a job, a community event, or even a simple act of kindness like being a shoulder to lean on in tough times for a friend or coworker.

Fact is, *how* you go about doing what you do is every bit as important as *what* you're doing. As Mac MacNally says, even if you currently have "a job that sucks" how you carry yourself, represent your nation, and represent who you genuinely are just may be the quickest way to a job that sucks way less.

EARNING THE BALL
VS. WANTING THE BALL

CHAPTER 4

Basketball is a team game, but often individual performances, particularly the plays at crucial game-changing moments, or last second, game-winning shots make seasons like March Madness live up to its name.

Those often become the defining moments of a collegiate player's legacy. They can also turn into the right play at the right time on a national stage, which propels them to the next level; maybe to the NBA, WNBA, or a future coaching job.

Players who make these plays at crucial moments in important games are always around the ball. More on this in Chapter 13, Be Around the Ball. Most of the time they actually have the ball in their hands. That's by design and for a reason. They've earned it. They've become the go-to man or woman in the most challenging, crucial, and important circumstances. If they execute, they will certainly get the notoriety, credit, fame, credibility and often the next opportunity. Why?

Because they made it happen. The team, the coach, the fans, and the organization counted on them, and they came through again.

But they had to earn it.

Everybody Wants it, but Few Earn it

Coaches draw up plays, leaning on certain players in crucial moments for a reason. Those players have earned the right to be the "go-to" team member. They came in early, before practice and worked on their game. They were diligent in the off-season, working out, staying in shape, and focusing on continuous improvement. They out-played, out-hustled, and out-performed everyone else on a regular basis in practice throughout the season. They do the little things at the routine Tuesday, Wednesday, or Thursday afternoon practice, which add up and prepare them for greatness. They earn the right to the ball in the final ten seconds of a nationally televised game. They deserve it. They earned the right. They work hard for the opportunity and then they follow-through and execute.

In life, in business, and in our careers we all want the ball. Everyone wants "to take the shot" that gets attention, credit, or leads to a better opportunity. Everyone wants the chance to make the decisions, be the boss, get the promotion, hold the pen, present to the top executives, and ultimately get the exposure. All of that will open doors to more opportunities including more money, stronger relationships, and even a better life.

Everybody wants it. The great ones, however, the great players, the amazing leaders, salespeople, the best teachers, professors, event planners, coordinators, and the best of the best move into the middle of the action, where the important stuff is happening because they earn it. They do little things in the off-season or on routine days when nobody is watching. They get the nod, the promotion, and the opportunities because they truly deserve it.

Simply Ask How You Can Earn It

I like best-selling author Mark Sanborn's definition of a leader. It's, ***"Anyone who accepts the challenge of influence."***

I like it because nowhere in that definition do you find a "title" that requires permission to lead. In fact, Sanborn wrote a book about the concept he calls, "You Don't Need a Title to be a Leader."

I highly recommend the book and the mindset. If you're 100 percent happy and content with your current job, life stage, or situation, then when you hit your knees tonight to pray before climbing into bed, thank the good Lord above for that blessing. *Pray for the rest of us if you don't mind because we all want that, too.*

On the other hand, do you find yourself making the commute to and from work wondering if you'll ever grow into a larger role with more responsibility, a better quality of life, and a bigger paycheck? Stop yourself from merely "craving it" and take action to earn it.

It takes being vulnerable and open with yourself to admit maybe you're not quite ready. Although 90 percent of the time you and everyone else knows you'll positively crush it. You see it, you feel it, and everyone around you recognizes it in a heartbeat. However, only a few of those people around you possess the keys to your next opportunity. Whether it's the next opening to lead a new project to showcase your talents or the next chance for a promotion, your boss and maybe his or her boss hold the keys. He or she makes the decision. Not "everyone else".

If you're like me, you may not agree with your bosses 100 percent of the time. In fact, you may not only disagree with them much of the time, but perhaps you're frustrated with them about certain situations, which never seem to improve. Like it or not, they're still the boss. They get to do boss things, including developing you as a team member, whether you agree with them or not.

Take an otherwise irritating situation, and manufacture a purposeful conversation around exactly what you need to do to "earn the ball." In a work environment full of prideful people all around, it takes courage to proactively bring up the topic with your leader.

While everyone else walks around pointing to their illustrious work and how awesome they are, what if you went to your boss and asked what you can do to help? What if you were the one person who asked for direct feedback on your work? Then, you double down, implementing and mastering the skills, traits, or disposition you need to improve in order to achieve the next level. You'd walk away from the conversation with a laser-focused game plan addressing exactly what you must do to earn the ball.

Executing Game Plans = Earning It

Now, all you must do is execute your game plan. It's no different than in Little League, basketball, football, soccer, or hockey when you were younger. Your teammates for whom all the big plays were drawn up, earned it. They earned it by flat-out, consistently executing their own or the coach's game plan.

What does "executing the game plan look like?" It's simple but not always easy to out execute everyone else, whether it's a competitor, a rival, or competing candidates for the next opportunity. Keep telling yourself successful people do things less successful people never want to do. It's about coming in early and staying late. It's about spending time each morning, afternoon, and evening thinking how you can be more efficient, do more with less, and add more value to people like your boss, your Guests or your clients. Even adding value to your family can make a difference and absolutely earn you the ball.

Following up with the same people for whom you've added value, sets you apart even more. Attentive comments from you show you're paying attention and that you care. Combine that with old-fashioned conversation, and those are the little things, which mean the most to people. That's precisely what makes you memorable or even remarkable.

Spend time with your leaders and peers, asking for direct, honest feedback on how you can earn the right for more:

- More responsibility
- More balance
- More opportunities
- And even more money

Then, simply execute the action plans you create from their feedback. If that doesn't set you apart, I don't know what will. Before you know it, bingo bango bongo, you'll find yourself facilitating the meeting instead of merely attending it. You'll be given the ball.

Whether it's the project, the opportunity, or the promotion, it'll be in your hands because you earned it.

For years, as a leader in the hospitality industry, from Orlando to Miami to Las Vegas to Southern California, I'd consistently do it better than the next person. I'd get to work earlier, I'd stay at work later, and I'd pour my heart not just into the daily work but also into the people. I built solid relationship after relationship with passion, a full heart, and leading with love all the way. Yet I always wondered if I'd ever grow out of middle management. I would over-rotate on why or how he or she got the executive job I absolutely knew I could perform better.

Chances are they earned it. They probably had opportunities for improvement earlier in their career, and enhanced them. I wanted it. I dreamed about it. I envisioned myself in those roles. However, I needed to do more of what I'm recommending you do. It would've served me well to spend more time and focus, seeking to understand from my bosses, what I needed to work on and improve to earn the next opportunity. Just like you and almost everyone else, I continue to be a work in progress, with my share of flaws.

If you find yourself with more thoughts of "wanting it" rather than thoughts of how you can "earn it," your pride and a big case of "woe is me" may be clouding your heart and mind. Unfortunately, it can also cloud your career.

There's nothing wrong with wanting it,
but the best way to get it is to earn it.

THE ATTRACTION OF WINNING AND AN UNDERLYING PARADOX

CHAPTER 5

Don't you love winning? Since those long, summer days playing and competing out on the playground, we're conditioned to win at all costs and bask in that amazing moment of "winning bliss" we all crave.

Back in the day when our team won a Little League game on a Saturday morning, the whole team would head over to the Shake Shop for ice cream. Even in my college days, if Florida Southern College won a home basketball game we all got pizza in the locker room after the game. Leaders in corporate America buy their teams doughnuts, coffee, or lunch if their team "wins" and achieves the goal for the week or month. Here we are today, living in a society – whether it's about sports or our careers, and we're obsessed with winning.

We see it in sports every year. The fans are a bit louder, they wear their team colors more often, and people watch their teams more frequently when they're winning. That's when it's easy to be a fan. It's way more fun.

The same logic applies at work. When it's our idea or when our point of view sways a boss's decision, or we get our way, we feel like we've won. It's almost as good as that blissful, winning feeling we had at ten years old on the playground. Somehow it resurfaces inside us in the conference room when everyone finally sees it our way. We feel good because winning is attractive. Who doesn't want to be attractive?

Why is "winning the argument" so attractive? Is it because for a split second you know and everyone else knows you were right?

While Not Everyone Wins, We All Have a Story

However, *winning* usually doesn't just happen. Quite the opposite is true. It takes steady, constant hard work to win once and then even more to win on a more consistent basis. That includes planning, studying, practicing, sacrificing, and executing. So many finite details must come together. Individual performances must be great, but they can't overshadow or prevent the *team* from delivering a collective *winning* effort.

Consider the hard work, sacrifice, and commitment required to win. It's not appealing or attractive, nor is it easy to do these things all the time. It's hard. Everyone wants to win, but not everyone has what it takes or is willing to do what it takes to win.

But everyone has a story.

Every person has a story of where they've been. They also have a story of where they're going. The more we learn about others, the more we learn about their stories including:

- What inspires them
- What motivates them
- How they approach their daily routine
- How they attack their goals, and
- Why they do what they do –

This is how you get to know people and their true character.

Another Olympics Thread...

You may recall in Chapter 3 I said I love the Olympics, we all do. We love it for the athletic competition, but there's an underlying pull to the stories of Olympians that keep us engaged during those 16 days of glory. We practically drink up their stories about:

- How they grew up,
- Where they trained,
- What inspired them, and
- How they overcame adversity

The stories of who the Olympians are on the inside bring their true character to light.

One Sunday morning, during the 2014 Winter Games in Sochi, I watched as Gracie Gold crushed it in the team figure skating competition. I know absolutely nothing about figure skating. As I watched I thought, "She nailed it." Every jump was flawless, and she was perfectly dialed in. While I was impressed with her skating, I couldn't help but be inspired by *her story*.

The commentators told the story of how she first tried on ice skates at a birthday party. They spoke about her rise to the top of the sport in recent years with a stunning performance at the national championships. I learned she was only 18-years old at the time, but moved all over, living in different cities, training to become the Olympian we know and love today. She made huge sacrifices, moving all the way from Michigan to Los Angeles to train with notable figure skating coach, Frank Carroll. She did it all as a young teen, leading up to the 2014 Winter Games in Sochi, Russia. Gold's sacrifice, commitment and hard work are inspiring.

After she skated, gracefully exited the ice and awaited her score, I turned off the TV. I went to church without even finding out if she won. I realized it didn't matter if her performance won the United States gold, silver, or bronze. I was so inspired by her story and the type of person I just learned she was, I forgot all about who was "winning or losing."

So, is it all about winning, or is there more to the story?

Is Winning Really the Attraction?
Or Is It Something Else?

We think we'll be awesome and everyone will love us. We think we'll be *more attractive* if we win. However, at the end of the day winning isn't nearly as attractive as your story. As with any story *characters* always make or break the storyline. Ultimately, they impact how good the story is or isn't. For all of us, our personal *character* makes or breaks our story and how inspiring and attractive it is for others when they hear it or when they encounter us – in conversation, through an email, by way of others' stories – at home and at work.

Instead of focusing on winning, consider focusing on *who you're becoming.*

People with true character, integrity and courage are attractive, regardless how many wins or losses they've experienced.

That's the underlying paradox.

I've already mentioned some of Andy Stanley's teaching and writing. I'll bring up another Stanley-ism here, because it further illustrates the underlying paradox of attraction. He has a four-part sermon series titled, "New Rules for Love, Sex, and Dating." Not only is it eye opening and enlightening spiritually, it also speaks to how taking personal accountability and responsibility for "who we're becoming" can and will completely change the game.

Here's the pearl: Andy encourages single people struggling with the mere thought of "being single" to simply take a year off dating, to focus on themselves. This may sound odd, a bit self-centered and counter-intuitive, but there's more. He encourages folks to take a year off dating to focus on who they're becoming. The powerful self-assessment question below changed my life. I hope it changes yours, personally or professionally. Here's the question:

Are you becoming the person you're looking for is looking for?

This can be applied to your personal dating life, or, your professional, dating life as you continuously look and pine after your dream job with your dream company.

"How" and "Who" for the Win

Wow! Consider that question and your reply for a second. Talk about the ultimate "ego-check." We spend so much time trying to "win" because we cling to the notion winning is so attractive – being right, being better looking than everyone else, getting the accolades, the promotions and the money. Then we wonder why we "can't find the love of our lives." We trudge into work each day wondering why our hard work isn't rewarded with promotions, raises, and the recognition we deserve. After all, we keep "winning" these little arguments or debates with coworkers, staff or the boss. I mean, isn't it obvious? Clearly you're:

- Smarter than the others.
- Better than everyone else.
- Crushing it compared to them.
- Winning at this "game."

If so, why does it feel like you never really win? Because none of it is as attractive as your true character you reveal along the way, for better or worse. The real attraction and win goes to great people.

What makes them great? Factors like their work ethic, drive, commitment and compassion for others. Their ability to connect with and inspire other people to be great are the attractive qualities every boss or significant other wants in their ideal employee or partner.

Remember, achieving your objective – at work or at home - is important, for sure. However, how you arrive at your destination is almost more important. So, next time you're in the conference room or boardroom, in a passionate, heated dialogue with a coworker, boss, client, or staff member, be cognizant of your tone. Be aware of what frustrates you, and intentional about how you temper what comes out of your mouth.

This is hard, because often times, you know you're right. You know you have the answer, the proof, and the right direction the team or organization needs to go. Don't let "the attraction of winning" the debate over shadow who you really are as a person, deep down. Who are you? Remember:

- You're smart.
- You're kind.
- You're passionate
  .

My inclination is, you're also compassionate. I know you are, or you wouldn't have picked up this book and read this far.

You may be surprised by the end of the conversation, the winner of the debate isn't nearly as cool or attractive as the person who remains calm, respectful, and understanding throughout the conversation. We'll unpack more about communication and conversation, later in Chapter 15. Grace and class during heated debates reveal true character.

Honestly, people with true character usually win.

BE A LEADER
AMONG YOUR PEERS

CHAPTER 6

Point Guards, Shortstops, Quarterbacks, and Middle Linebackers among a few other "position players" are often leaders among their peers. They're not just extensions of the coach on the floor or field during their playing days of middle school, high school, college, or even the pros. But they also often become leaders, coaches, managers, and in some cases even executives in corporate offices, in sports or other industries.

Lead Before You're Expected to Lead

All leaders, at any level and in any setting whether its sports, business, or otherwise, became recognized as "The Leader" because they were first a leader among their peers. In sports, the "key players" on the team become Team Captains, the leaders among their teammates.

The same is true in our careers and in our lives. Key "go to" people who ultimately become the leaders of teams, then directors of divisions, then vice presidents of functions including Sales, Finance, Marketing, Operations, Human Resources and all the way to the C-Suite don't get there by chance. They got there by first becoming a leader among their peers. That is, they were a leader for years before they were given the title. They didn't have to be given permission to lead, instead they took on the responsibility and the challenge to lead. As presented in Chapter 5, being magnetically attractive often positions you in a more positive light with hiring leaders and executives who are paying attention. That's never a bad thing.

So how do you become a "leader among your peers?" Simple. The quickest way to become a leader among your peers is be the one person who always makes it all about their peers.

Make it About Them

In the early 2000's, I sat in a Leadership Development class at Disney University, at the *Walt Disney World*® Resort in Orlando, FL, excited, nervous, and anxious to be starting a new leadership role on the Grand Opening Team of one of Disney's new resorts. The facilitators paused the class and set their content aside. They welcomed in a guest speaker, one of the General Managers from another Disney resort. What he said about leadership back then, on that day, has stuck with me every day since.

He first congratulated us. After all everyone in the room was recently promoted into a leadership role for the first time, or, had just started with the company as a leader, coming from the outside as an external hire. He genuinely told us, "Congratulations! You've all been recognized as people who get the job done. You've been great doers. Now, you are leaders, you're leading other people. So now, it's less about what you do yourself, and instead it's all about how well you take a group of people, turn them into a functioning team, and lead them to do something."

Leadership is all about encouraging and inspiring people.

Leadership is all about encouraging and inspiring people. Those who become great at "making it about their team" as opposed to being all about themselves rise to become those key, "go to" people we all know, love, and trust as our leaders.

You might say to yourself, "Okay, great. Sounds good. To be a leader, to get the promotion and finally be recognized for my awesomeness, I must make it about "them" not me. What does that look like?"

The "I Think" Trap

For starters, consider one of the most overused phrases in the corporate world and maybe even in the world, in general, "I think…"

How often do we hear it? Partners, leaders, colleagues, and even our guests, customers, and clients say it all day long, day in and day out.

The risk of beginning a sentence with "I think" is that it assumes the person on the other end of the phone conversation, across the conference room table, across the aisle, in the audience, or in the classroom cares about what we think. It assumes we're already a respected and/or credible source of knowledge, on any given topic.

The truth is, they may not even care. Even worse, they may not even respect us, let alone what we think.

To emerge as a true leader among your peers, especially for those who take pride in the idea and challenge of leading, even before you get THE title, simply change the "I think…" to "What do you think?" in conversation with your peers.

The word "leadership" can be defined in many ways, but I like this one:

"Leadership is the activity of influencing people to cooperate towards a goal, which they come to find desirable and which motivates them over the long haul."

This quote is from Ordway Tead, author of "The Art of Influence."

Most people become successful because once upon a time, they were extremely talented. Whether it's selling, creating art of any kind, speaking, writing, dancing, or adding and subtracting; they crush it. Some people are excellent at doing, whatever they do.

For true leaders however, everything changes. It's less about what we do, and it becomes all about what we can inspire others to do. It's far less about what we think, and all about inspiring them to not only share what they think, but also to put their thoughts into action.

Once we accept that ever-so-dynamic (and at times difficult) challenge of influencing, it's less and less about us and ALL about them. The mark of a great leader, coach, teacher or mentor - those who accept, with an open mind and heart, the challenge of positive influence - is no longer about what they, themselves, can do. Instead it's all about how well they can lead and inspire others to go do *fill-in-the-blank* thing.

Great leaders facilitate open, collaborative conversations rather than dominating every conversation. More on *conversations* later in Chapter 15. Successful coaches take suggestions and input from their players and assistant coaches rather than taking a "my way or the highway" approach. Incredibly inspiring teachers and professors take pride in being lifelong learners. They take time to stop and ask students what they think as opposed to constantly pontificating, opening sentences with, "I think."

Making it all about *them* is the quickest way to gain respect and credibility. With respect and credibility comes trust from not only your peer group, but also and perhaps even more importantly for your career growth, your boss. When your own leaders know you've earned the trust of your peers, you suddenly become a front-runner in the candidacy for the next leadership or managerial opening. Your leaders know better than anyone, to lead people effectively, a leader must have credibility and respect among their team members.

Captains Steer 'Ships

Coaches in sports often leave it up to the team to vote on which player will be Team Captain. Consider some of the greatest Team Captains in the history of sports; famous ones or even those "captains" you loved when you were little, playing your sport, growing up. The Team Captains who come to mind likely had the respect of most, if not all the players. How do Captains gain credibility? How do they keep our respect, making it easy for us to trust them?

Captains of any team – sports teams, work teams, or otherwise steer 'SHIPS...

LeaderSHIP

Above all else, true captains must be leaders. They don't need to be "bossy," just leaders. Most of the time, the captains who emerge are not even defined by title, but instead they lead by example. Regardless of their official "title" leaders LEAD – they Listen, Educate, take Action, and Deliver for their teammates.

RelationSHIPs

Consider the Team Captains on your favorite sports teams. Watch them and notice the connections they have with coaches, teammates, fans, and even the media. It's apparent they spend time fostering relationships with people around them. That's one of the reasons so many people gravitate toward them, respecting them as team captains.

PartnerSHIPs

Captains realize, despite their superior talent, they can't do it alone. They're never afraid to rely on their partners. Russell Wilson, Super Bowl Champion Quarterback for the Seattle Seahawks, must trust his offensive line to protect him. When plays break down, he trusts his teammates to step up, improvise, and make plays, because he simply can't win football games by himself. The team is essential. Captains understand the importance of maximizing true partnerships resulting from meaningful, productive relationships they foster with teammates.

FellowSHIP, FriendSHIP and CompanionSHIP

Think about the most likeable people in your contact list on your phone, right now. Think about the most inspiring leaders you've ever known. Consider your most trusted partners at work. Chances are, the people who come to mind make a point of developing a sense of community with those around them. They don't lead through fear or power. Instead, they gain credibility and admiration because of their compassion and genuine interest in other people. With credibility and admiration comes likeability, and a person's likeability makes them someone worthy of following.

StewardSHIP

Perhaps this one doesn't come to mind as often as the other "SHIPs" listed above.

I love this Merriam-Webster definition of stewardship:

The conducting, supervising, or managing of something; the careful and responsible management of something entrusted to one's care."

True captains understand it's not all about them. They know and understand the very team or organization they're captaining doesn't even belong to them. That's what makes them special. While they understand "it" doesn't belong to them, whether it's the team, the office, the building, the company, the situation, or the project; they step up and take full responsibility anyway, as if it were their own.

This is perhaps the secret, which any great leader, coach, pastor, professor or teacher would tell us made them successful. To be great is to put the team, the organization, and the best interest of everyone else above one's personal agenda, fame, or fortune.

Putting the needs of your peers above your own and making it all about them may not make you CEO tomorrow. However, loving them, serving them and leading your peers today will certainly keep you moving toward the life and career you're dreaming about for tomorrow.

PART TWO

LISTEN TO YOUR COACHES

DEMYSTIFYING THE
LOST ART OF LISTENING

CHAPTER 7

I was about eleven years old, in my last year of Little League. I played shortstop and occasionally pitched (but not well). One Saturday morning I was on the mound pitching. My coach gave the sign to throw a change-up after I was throwing fastballs all game long. The hope was for the hitter to be out in front of a slower, change-up pitch, swing, and miss, of course. Instead, when I took a little off the pitch, the batter smacked it deep into the right field gap.

We May Not Know Everything After All

Frustrated, getting the ball back from a teammate, now with a runner on base, I kicked a few pebbles, slammed the ball into my glove, and mumbled under my breath, "Why can't I just throw the ball?"

From the corner of the dugout a low, stern voice called out, "'Cause I'm the coach. That's why."

At the ripe age of eleven I undoubtedly believed I knew everything there was to know about everything. I guess I saw myself as such a prodigy and student of the game, I knew more than the coach. Okay, no. Hardly.

I was a terrible pitcher, and not even very good at baseball. Maybe I was a decent shortstop, but I couldn't hit a lick. Pretty sure the coach, an adult my parents' age, and a great man in our community, might be a smidge more qualified to make the call. After all, he was the coach. It would've been wise to listen more and talk less; a lesson that applies just as much today as it did then.

Jimmy Buffett covers a song originally released by Fred Neil in the 60's, "Everybody's Talkin'." The first line is a microcosm of today's business world, and society, for that matter:

"Everybody's talkin' at me...
can't hear a word they're sayin'...
Only the echoes of my mind...

How often do you find yourself talking (or trying to talk) to someone, on the phone, videoconference, or during an in-person conversation, and you can't get a word in edgewise? Why? Because, uh, they won't stop talking. It's true. Everybody's always talking. Since they're always talking, we sit around chasing our thoughts and all we literally hear are "the echoes of our mind," a la Fred Neil's lyric.

How often do you leave your office, hop in your car, turn on the radio, get five miles down the road and have no idea what songs, commercials, or talk radio segments just played in the very car in which you're the only passenger? Maybe I'm the only one, but does your mind race with to-do's, concerns and fears weighing down every thought?

I'm sure you work or live with people who talk and talk and rarely pause to listen. It's a total thing and a bit of an epidemic plaguing corporate America. Grand Canyon size wedges are driven smack dab in the middle of relationships. It also prevents talented up and comers from "becoming" all they could, should, and would be, if only they'd listen. Unfortunately, it also keeps many from experiencing the levels of fulfillment and happiness they long for both at work and at home.

I'm just as guilty, having contributed to the epidemic here and there, not listening to a coach or two or a boss or three in the past. I'm embarrassed to admit maybe on a few occasions I'm guilty of not even listening to my parents, friends, or significant others. However, I'm a work in progress, like everyone else. Nobody's perfect. I think I'm better now than I was in the past. I share this with you because I want you to have fewer annoying days and many more happy, fulfilling ones.

What makes a day fulfilling or annoying? We can all agree annoying days are filled with one gross encounter after another. Some guy or girl is a jerk, disrespecting us, our team, or our family and friends. What about people who act like know-it-alls, pontificating, rambling on with their opinions, never thinking to ask for ours? They think they know, but bless their hearts, they have no clue. They don't understand, and rarely stop to take a few minutes to learn the realities of a situation.

On the other hand, consider an environment filled with respect, learning, understanding and love. How does that sound to you? That's the type of environment you can cultivate within your teams, companies, families, and relationships when and if you listen.

Don't fall into the "know it all" trap. Of course, you're smart. Be smart enough to realize someone else might know something, too. My wife is six years younger than me. Back when we were dating we had a few "fights." Nothing major, just typical squabbles. One of my best friends gave me some great advice, as I was in mid-argument with the wonderful woman who is now my wife. He said, "Be open to listening to her. You might learn something."

He was right then, and he continues to be right even today. I thought since I was "the older one" I automatically knew best. Dumb. Wrong. Not even close. I'm so glad I learned that lesson early in our relationship journey. If I didn't learn to listen and become open to new ideas and perspectives, we probably wouldn't have progressed in our relationship or ever even married. That's a scary thought.

Listening is Respectful

Listening is the ultimate display of respect. It says they matter more than we do. Their problem is bigger and more important, right now, than anything else. Intently, actively listening makes people feel special as opposed to an afterthought.

Countless times I've talked to a leader or executive, and as I'm talking they put me on hold or pause. It's like they're pausing their TV at home so they can answer another call, talk over me, or give their final word with no regard for what I'm sharing. Nothing turns me off more, and nothing makes me want to work for them less.

If you're a leader, gaining the respect of those you lead is almost a prerequisite to earning the right to lead or coach on anything of importance. Listening is the quickest way to earn respect. Not listening is the quickest way to get nowhere fast with any individual or team.

Be quicker to listen than you speak, and gain the respect of your team, coworkers, bosses, and most importantly, your friends and family. Your days will have less tension and strife and more meaningful, productive conversations.

Listening is Learning

Often the difference between feeling fulfilled at work and feeling empty, lost, annoyed, and burned out is all about whether or not you're learning anything. This is another reason to listen. It's amazing how much more you learn when you pause, quiet your mind, and listen to what others say. This is true for peers to your left and right as well as the very teams you lead.

Sometimes it's hard to listen to your boss or an executive, especially if you don't agree 100 percent of the time. In some cases, you may not even like them. I get it. Remember, they're in their roles for a reason, and they just might know a few things. Be open and willing to listen to what they say. You may not agree with everything you hear, but at least you listened. Even if you don't agree with what they say or how they say it, you've learned what not to do or how not to say it.

The key is you're learning. If you want to continue to grow, and you're focused on who you're becoming, it's imperative you take every opportunity to learn new things daily. A great way to increase your chances of learning every day is to simply listen.

Listen to Understand

How awesome is it when people give us their solutions to the company's problems or even our own problems, yet they don't understand the problem for which they've just outlined a solution? Not very awesome. It's gross. In those instances, it's obvious. They. Clearly. Were. Not. Listening!

This is another compelling reason to listen. When you make a point to listen attentively, you begin understanding with more clarity. When you have a clear understanding, you have less doubt, fewer questions to chase down, and a clearer picture of the situation. Once you have a clearer understanding, you can provide viable solutions, fresh perspectives, and help solve problems. It's hard to solve problems for people unless you understand the situation, and you cannot understand situations unless or until you follow the wise advice of Vanilla Ice, and stop, collaborate, and listen.

Your ability and willingness to solve problems, especially your boss's problems, is directly correlated to the probability you could be tapped on the shoulder for growth opportunities and promotions going forward. More reason to listen.

Listening is Loving

Think about the people you love most. No really, think about them now. Why do you love them? Why are they important to you? You love them because they respect you, they've taught you things, they "get you," they understand, and they love you back.

You may think, "Those are four compelling reasons to listen, but it's hard to pull off. It's hard to listen when I have so much on my plate." I agree. It's harder and harder nowadays, especially with how connected we stay all day, night and throughout the weekend. Emails don't stop like they used to, and the computer we used to log into at work to receive emails is now in your pocket or purse. Far too often it ends up on the dining room table during dinner we're supposed to be sharing with our loved ones. Or, it lights up, buzzing away on the coffee table while trying to enjoy an evening show with your roommates or significant other.

Listening Isn't So Hard After All

Here are four ideas, to help you with the elusive, lost art of listening:

- **Find a time and place to get quiet and turn off the "echoes of your mind."** When you force yourself to turn off the phone, radio, TV, or mental voices in your head, it helps clear out the cobwebs. Shut off what many call the "monkey chatter" in your brain. You'll find you're able to listen when it's time to do so – with your spouse, partner, boss, friend, or client.

- **Pray. Ask your higher power for guidance, direction, and patience.** This is a hard thing. So, of course we should pray for how best to handle hard situations. Notice how this step comes after *finding a place to get quiet.* Sometimes we can be quick to pray but so slow to listen to the guidance and comfort, which comes to us from Him. Once you find your time to get quiet, pray for help. Then, be ready for the nudge from above. If you're not careful, you'll miss it. But if you're intentional about asking, quiet enough to hear it, and faithful enough to trust it, you'll be fine.

- **Try not to ignore or dismiss people with differing views from your own.** We're so accustomed to our smart phones and social media we get used to scrolling past a dumb post or hit ignore when an unwelcome incoming call lights up your phone. Unfortunately, you can't do that in real life with real people. If you find yourself in an awkward situation, disagreeing with another person's opinion, let them get it out. There's no rule forcing you to agree, argue or even respond to them. Simply listen. If nothing else, you're being respectful and gaining an understanding of their perspective. They probably enjoy getting it off their chest, and you might even learn something.

- **Put down your phone when they talk**. I know. I'm guilty too. We can't possibly think we're smart enough, dynamic enough or charismatic enough to keep up with our FB, Instagram, Twitter, multiple text threads, company email, personal email, and our Watch ESPN app. All this while trying to have an engaging, meaningful conversation with a coworker, spouse, friend, boss, or client. Literally not possible.

You're smart, but not that smart. You're a human being, and so are they. They're telling you something either because they need someone to talk to or because they value your opinion. If it's your boss, they're telling you something because they're expecting you to get 'er done. If you look at your phone while they talk, you run the risk of hurting their feelings or hurting your credibility as a friend, family member, or even that dynamic, high performer at work.

If you find yourself stuck in the hamster wheel, with more upsetting days than fulfilling ones, there's a better way. Better days are around the corner. Be the one who listens and:

- Become known as the respectful one,
- Learn all kinds of new stuff,
- Begin to understand things you never understood before, and
- Receive an abundance of love from people to your left and right, your team, and even your boss.
- Replace irritating days with fulfilling ones because you listen.

Are you thinking these points seem rather basic? You're spot on. Listening to others is just one of many small, yet critical fundamentals we can forget about in our technology-obsessed world which sets high performers apart from their peers.

There's more to discover about the wisdom of handling fundamentals consistently in the next chapter. No, seriously. Turn the page. The "fundamentals chapter" tips off with a great John Wooden quote. See you there.

FUNDAMENTALS MATTER –
WIN WITH SMALL, CONSISTENT PLAYS

CHAPTER 8

"I discovered early on the player who learned the fundamentals of basketball will have a much better chance of succeeding and rising through the levels of competition than a player who is content to do things his own way. A player should be interested in learning why things are done a certain way. The reasons behind the teaching often go a long way to helping develop the skill."
~ John Wooden
11-Time NCCAA Championship
Coach of the UCLA Bruins

We could probably end this chapter right here, with a walk-off, mic drop quote like this on fundamentals from the late, great Coach John Wooden. Sure, a word like this, even the thought of topics like "fundamentals" isn't exactly sexy. The thought of adhering to the fundamentals of anything isn't always 100 percent fun, 100 percent of the time.

It was a hot sunny, summer day in the mid-1990's, and I was on the outdoor basketball courts at the University of Kentucky Wildcat Basketball Camp. After lunch each day was the best. That's when the most heated scrimmage games of the whole week, literally and figuratively, happened. It was my favorite part of camp, actually playing. I caught the ball on an outlet pass and headed for the middle of the court, full speed ahead. My team had a three-on-one fast break, and I had the rock. For anyone who's ever played hoops, especially in the summertime on outdoor courts, you know this is basketball euphoria at its finest.

For a split-second I embodied Magic Johnson, and put down a couple dribbles moving up the floor. I looked left and threw a wrap-around, behind the back pass to my teammate who I thought for sure was making a mad dash to the hoop. I just knew my moves were going to be an absolute highlight, and quite possibly win me the Most Valuable Player award for the week.

Instead, my teammate didn't come close to making a mad dash anywhere. My Showtime, behind-the-back pass in the open court I thought would become a Sports Center worthy highlight, ended up sailing into the adjacent basketball court, stopping play on another game. Awesome. Not.

After a quick clap, slap on the butt, and a "my bad" to my teammate, one of the coaches, in his coach voice, said, "Make easy plays, young man. Easy plays. Small, consistent plays win in the long run."

Got it. Oops. No highlight. No MVP award.

But I learned something, because after all, it makes sense. If you chart sports history, from basketball to baseball to soccer, football, hockey, lacrosse, volleyball, and every sport in between, the most successful teams and the most successful players have been and continue to be fundamentally sound.

By the same token, if you chart the historical business successes from Wall Street to Main Street, over the years, you'd see the same thing. The most successful companies and organizations are those whose teams were and continue to be faithful to the fundamentals of their individual roles, and, what it takes to be successful in their respective industries.

Nail the Fundamentals First

It's easy to get caught up in the excitement of what could be a game-changing, earth-shattering, blockbuster new idea. We find ourselves in our boss's office, on the phone with the corporate office, or even in the aisles and hallways talking with peers about how much better it would be if we just did XYZ.

Sometimes those "XYZ" ideas sound good, and they probably would even add value and make a huge impact, if all the stars aligned at the same time, in the right way. Just like my "almost" Sports Center highlight, behind-the-back pass would've been amazing if it worked. But are those ideas or strategies feasible right now? Are they things you can control, right now, today? Usually not. Especially if you work for a huge corporation, you know how hard it is to move the seemingly immovable mountains it would take to implement your game-changing, behind-the-back pass idea.

I'm not saying give up on all your ideas. I would never suggest you shy away from offering innovative proposals to leaders, peers, and executives to make things better. I'm simply submitting those things may take time, strategic planning, and tactical conversation to be implemented. In the meantime, you can do what your coaches always encouraged you to do, stick to the essentials. Fundamentals in sports may be things like;

- Stay low,
- Move your feet,
- Communicate with each other,
- Backspin,
- Arch,
- Follow through,
- Watch the ball,
- See the field, or
- See the court.

In our careers, regardless of the business or industry, we have fundamentals, which we can control ourselves, without moving mountains of corporate corporateness. While those game changing ideas are good ones and will probably be amazing one day, it's also amazing how much value you can create today, by simply and consistently implementing the fundamentals well.

Do Simple Better

Joe Maddon, Manager for the 2016 World Series Champion, Chicago Cubs made the following phrase famous during the Cubs' magical run to a championship, "Do simple better." The Cubbies, in 2016 were sexy, young, talented, fun, and even flashy at times. However, at the end of the day, they flat out executed, day in and day out, and won more games than any other team in Major League Baseball during the 2016 season. They did it with fundamentals "doing simple better" and, embodying another Joe Maddon-ism, which was "try not to suck."

Hitters hit groundballs and got on base. More hitters hit more ground balls, and drove in runs. In the field, they caught the ball, threw the ball with accuracy, and pitchers threw strikes, for nine innings every game. Sometimes it took extra innings, but they simply "did simple better" and more consistently than any other team in Major League Baseball in 2016.

What do the "fundamentals" look like for you, in your job today? Chances are, while we all have different roles with much different companies, some of the following fundamentals apply across the board:

- Be on time. In fact, be early.
- Prepare in advance for a big call, meeting or big day. Know your stuff.
- If you're a leader, know your people, know your numbers, and be yourself. Being real and authentic is who we are, yet so many think they must constantly be someone they're not at work. Just be you, real, and genuine.
- Write emails using a consistent, intelligent and professional voice.
- Respond to emails, voicemails, and text messages in a timely manner.

- Have a Daily Game Plan with winning tactics specific to your role.
- Execute said Daily Game Plan every single day, without fail.
- Time management is crucial. Spend the most time on what's most valuable.
- Trust your processes. They were set up for specific reasons to get things done. They probably were tested over time as well.
- If you don't agree with the process, create a new one, shop it and implement.

These fundamentals sound simple, but when executed consistently, you win, and your team wins.

We'll wrap up this chapter with another favorite John Wooden quote. Very fundamental in nature, it can be applied to any job, on any level, in any industry. Wooden said, *"Be quick, but not in a hurry."*

"Be quick, but not in a hurry."

BELIEVE YOU BELONG

CHAPTER 9

*"No one can make you feel inferior
without your consent."*

~ Eleanor Roosevelt

Kentucky and basketball; they're like peanut butter and jelly or coffee and cream. Certain pairings just work well together. I grew up watching, loving, studying, practicing, and playing basketball as much as possible. Basketball played a primary role growing up and still does.

My fondest basketball memories happened in the offseason, during the summer. I went to three or four outstanding basketball camps each year. If you're an athlete or former athlete, you probably did the same thing throughout the off-season for your sport as well.

Never Think of Yourself as a Second Class Player

The summer between my junior and senior year of high school, I was selected to play on the Kentucky Junior All-Star Team. It was a huge honor. We had to prepare for two tournaments; one in Louisville, KY and another in Las Vegas, NV. So, the "All-Stars" spent a week at an invitation only basketball camp called "Hoop Stars."

I remember being incredibly excited and nervous all wrapped up in a ball of enthusiasm. An invitation to a camp like this was a goal throughout much of my childhood. I looked up to many former Kentucky Jr. All-Stars. Often, I dreamed of getting the opportunity to play with the best of the best in Kentucky. Then my fantasy went even further, to play against the best of the best from around the country.

Mostly I wanted the tee shirt that read, "Kentucky Jr. All-Stars" in big, bold BLUE letters across the chest. I was 16 when I received that coveted tee shirt. I kept it well into my twenties. Admittedly, the only reason I don't have it today is because it literally started disintegrating after years of wearing and washing.

Luckily, my high school basketball coach, Charles Baker, was one of the Kentucky Jr. All-Star Team coaches. He was at Hoop Stars Camp that week. I ran into Coach Baker around the campus grounds on the second day of the week. I was playing with and getting to know many of the All-Stars from around the state. I told Coach about "this guy from Lexington Catholic" and "that other guy from Louisville Eastern." I was describing how effortlessly they seemed to dunk the ball, their quickness, and ability to score at will. Coach listened patiently, as we walked and talked. As usual, I did most of the talking.

Finally, Coach gave me some advice, at age 16 at Hoop Stars Basketball Camp on the campus of Eastern Kentucky University. I've taken his advice with me everywhere I go. I'll continue taking his wise words with me. It's so valuable I'm passing it along to you to carry with you wherever you go in life.

We both paused and leaned up against a railing overlooking one of the basketball courts. He stopped me and said, "Hey, don't be so in awe of these guys. Never think of yourself as second-class. You can play, and you belong here, with everyone else. Believe you belong."

BOOM! Once he said those words it totally shifted my perspective. I went from playing *just okay* to having one of the most outstanding basketball weeks of my high school career. In an instant, my game caught fire with confidence and courage. It was as if I flipped a switch and my feelings shifted from inferior to feeling as confident as ever. He was right.

For the rest of my week at Hoop Stars camp and during the tournaments that summer, I hustled, took charges, dove after loose balls, and played hard. I just played all out. It was "you only live once" kind of play. I had an awesome time, loosened up, and leaned into my skills, talent, and my passion for the game. I wasn't shy about pulling up for jump shots right off the dribble as if I was Michael Jordan. I had a blast, directing traffic as a point guard with so many talented guys on the court playing with me. I competed at my best, once I started believing I belonged out there with the rest of the Kentucky Jr. All Stars. It made a world of difference in my basketball game and in the game of life.

Years later, in my first leadership role as a Housekeeping Manager at a big, fine resort in Orlando, I was the youngest manager by close to a decade. I was barely 21 years old, walking in and out of meetings with people who had worked in the hospitality industry for two or three decades. Then, I transitioned from Hotel Operations to Sales and Marketing. Working in a more corporate setting, I'd walk into meetings with Vice Presidents, Directors and the like at Disney®, in big, elegant conference rooms and boardrooms.

I began traveling, crisscrossing the country, representing Disney Parks & Resorts. I built relationships with client companies and sold the magic of Disney® through their theme park tickets. Only in my early 20's, I was attending fancy dinners, lunches and golf matches with "big time executives" from "big time" companies.

Several years down the road, I left Disney® to attend Cornell University for my graduate work, in the big, bad, prestigious Ivy League. After graduate school, I landed a Director position in Las Vegas at the 5-Star, 5-Diamond, Wynn-Encore Las Vegas where I worked for Mr. Wynn. I joined his talented team of executives as we served and played host to celebrities, millionaires, billionaires, and people who arrived from around the globe. In my next move, I found myself sitting in the executive boardroom at the brand-new

Cosmopolitan of Las Vegas. I helped build the team and create the culture of what became a game-changing new, unique resort smack dab in the middle of the Vegas strip.

I'm not sharing my resume to brag. I tell you about those career moves and seasons of my life because at every step I heard Coach Baker saying, "Don't think of yourself as second-class; believe you belong."

A little fella from Eastern Kentucky, I'll always be. But I discovered people from fancy places aren't better than me, smarter than me, and nor do they belong more than me.

The same goes for you. Never think of yourself as second class.

Wherever you are, wherever you're from, and wherever you're going; no matter how rough, tough, or intimidating the circumstances, *always think of yourself as a first-class player.* Believe you belong. The fact that you

"always think of yourself as a first-class player"

bought this book, and especially because you're reading it tells me you possess passion, drive and a desire to learn, grow, win, and be happy. (Thank you. I hope you're enjoying the conversation as much as I am.)

You're already winning. Why? Because most people in your company, on your team or in your community are watching Seinfeld reruns, binge watching House of Cards or Orange is the New Black on Netflix right now. What are you doing?

- You're reading.
- You're improving.
- You're growing.

I believe you'll be a game changer for people (*including your annoying boss*), and make their life better. In the process of doing so, you'll be rewarded, and enjoy much success. I know it. Deep down inside you know it, too. I just wanted to remind you.

Believe you belong.

You're Enough

You are enough. You do belong. Lean into your skills, talents, and drive. Always think of yourself as a first-class player. God created you, uniquely and perfectly in his image. Remember that. Remember who you are. Everybody has "stuff." I know you've had your fair share of stuff. We all have.

Consider the question: what pulled you through those nerve-racking moments and tough seasons earlier in your life? It was your faith and your character that saw you through. Your faith and character will see you through the next dollop of stuff, whatever it turns out to be, as well.

So be confident. Believe you belong, wherever you go in life.

Live for an Audience of One

Here's another golden nugget I'll pass along. When I first heard this phrase at Central Christian Church in fabulous Las Vegas, it completely changed the game and all "the games" since for me. I hope this idea changes you, for the better, as it did for me. I learned this concise yet powerful idea from Senior Pastor, Jud Wilhite. It gave me the confidence to pursue anything, anywhere, at any time. Even writing this book.

It'll give you the confidence to just be you, only better. No more will you worry about what others might say if you fail, or if they judge you. Here it is:

Live for an audience of one.

God created us perfectly, in His image. He is always there for us - yesterday, today, and tomorrow. He'll never stop loving us, even when we fall short. He'll never stop pursuing us, despite our habits and hang-ups, which make everyone less than perfect. He knows you're not perfect. It's okay to not be okay in God's eyes. Even if your boss thinks you're not good enough, God loves you all the same.

Even if our guests, customers, and clients think we're weird or not up to their standards, they really aren't the most important judges.

For me playing against bigger, faster, stronger competition on the basketball court shook my confidence back in the day. Later in my career, it was big, bad senior leaders and executives in corporate America. I'll be honest they occasionally rattled my cage. Sometimes they made me feel like a nervous wreck and a fish out of water.

I'm not sure what gets in your head, or what shakes your confidence, but remember that simple, powerful concept; *live and work for an audience of one*. Because after all, only He decides when it's time to wrap up our short time here on Earth. It won't matter what the boss or the court of public opinion thinks. It won't even matter what your friends and family think. It only matters what God thinks.

I'm sure there are times when you feel like a complete mess. It's okay. Chapter 10 coming right up is all about letting others see your professional maturity on the outside even if you don't always feel that way on the inside. We may be a mess half the time, but happily, we're God's mess.

The ultimate Bible verse for buoying up your confidence, in anything, anytime, and anywhere is Romans 8:31,

"If God is for us, who could be against us."

Wherever you are, and wherever you go, *believe you belong*. God had something to do with why you're there. He's working in you and through you all the time. Always think of yourself as a first-class player. Be confident, and believe 100 percent that you belong.

REVEAL CHARACTER – SHOW YOUR PROFESSIONAL MATURITY

CHAPTER 10

We heard it often while growing up…all the ways we were supposedly *"building character."* Remember the days when you:

- Lost a Little League game.
- Got a bad grade on a test.
- Brought home a substandard report card.
- Got in trouble.
- Got disciplined.
- Suffered through an embarrassment.

You probably heard the words, "That's okay, it'll build your character."

What about now?

Now you're grown up. You're no longer in Little League. You're even well beyond high school. Over the years, you learned right from wrong, and you've been embarrassed at one time or another. Everyone goes through it.

The Days of Building Character Are Over

When "things happen" as an adult you:

- Lose the argument,
- Encounter adversity (at work or at home)
- Are left feeling embarrassed

Are you still building character? Maybe in some cases. But as adults; as leaders, coaches, bosses, business partners, friends, family, neighbors, coworkers and significant others when put to the test, whether it's in your personal life or at work, you have an opportunity to reveal *your character*.

A Merriam-Webster dictionary definition of the word, *character* is:

noun \ˈker-ik-tər, ˈka-rik-\

"The way someone thinks, feels, and behaves: someone's personality."

These are the moments that speak volumes. They show you and everyone else who you genuinely are, on the inside, and just what a strong a person you've become.

The OneMoreStep opportunity here is realizing around every turn, in any season, you have a chance to reveal your true character; especially in times of distress, adversity, or, when you're uncomfortable and seriously out of your comfort zone. You discover what you're made of and "who you are" now; in your adult season of life. Everyone else who notices also discovers who you are in these important moments of truth. If you can learn to manage your emotions in these awkward, annoying moments, you'll continue setting yourself apart from the pack.

When your true character is revealed, how you think, feel, and behave outwardly might make a positive difference in someone's life.

Or, it could have a negative impact on others around you. The good news is what gets revealed is absolutely up to you. You get to choose.

Undefeated – It's About Character

I love the 2011 documentary film, "Undefeated", which chronicles the struggles of a high school football team over the years in Memphis, Tennessee.

Coach Bill Courtney, the Manassas Tigers Head Football Coach, started coaching the film's featured group of senior players when they were all in the eighth grade. While it's exciting and cool to watch what Coach Bill did with the Tigers on the football field, what makes the film inspiring isn't about football at all. It's about character.

"Character is the will to do what's right even when it's hard."

- Andy Stanley

I recommend Coach Bill Courtney's book, Against the Grain: A Coach's Wisdom on Character, Faith, Family, and Love, to anyone, at any stage in their life or career. Coach Bill challenges his readers to become *uncommon men and women*. The principles and illustrations in the book will leave you inspired to take a deep breath and faithfully be just that, uncommon.

It seems counter-intuitive. Some of the most telling, character-revealing moments in life are when you realize you're wrong. You made a mistake. Or, you just plain messed up. I've had more of these moments than I care to admit. Hopefully, I don't make the same mistake twice. Another one of my favorite authors, Mark Sanborn, says to understand adults all you must do is understand children. Isn't that the truth?

What do you do when you realize you've made a mistake? What do your first gut reactions or instincts tell you? How do you react? And, who's the first to blame? Actually, who's the last person you typically blame? I'm no different than you. Most people are incredibly quick to blame others and have perfected the art of making excuses. The person in the mirror is often the last person at the end of the line we consider blaming for anything.

A Funny Story about Blame

I was on a Southwest Air flight from Orange County, California to Louisville, Kentucky with a stopover in Las Vegas, Nevada. That's a fun little thread, because at one time or another in my life, I've called each of these states home. I was on the same plane all the way through, so I remained seated while the Orange County people exited the plane in Vegas.

The passenger in the seat directly across the aisle from me couldn't believe it. He called the flight attendant over and with a concerned, yet highly annoyed tone he asked the flight attendant, "What did you do with my bag?"

The flight attendant was taken aback as she explained they normally don't move people's bags once they're stowed away in the overhead bins.

The fella in 11B was adamant, insisting, "Somebody moved my bag."

An awkward, five-minute dialogue of, "I thought I saw…"

"Who moved what?" and

"Guess you'll have to check with the gate agent as you exit to see if somebody else grabbed your bag," ensued.

He stormed off the plane as the flight attendant and I checked all around, asking him if this one was his or what about this blue one?

Nope, his bag was black, he snarled.

My flight was delayed; so I had time to step off the plane, grab a bag of Combos, some peanuts, and a Smart Water. The breakfast of champions, because it was too early for a sandwich. Plus, I knew a nice meal with Mom and Dad was waiting for me as soon as I landed in Louisville. As I ate my snack and charged my laptop just outside the gate, I saw Mr. 11B, rolling his blue carry-on bag right down the C concourse at Las Vegas McCarran Airport! I gave him a, "You found it!" and a high-five.

He replied, "Yeah, they had it for me."

I was in a great mood that morning so I cracked up and said, "Dude, that was on the plane in the overhead bin above us. That's the bag we asked you about!"

He cracked up too, and we shared a nice laugh in front of gate C21. He finally owned up to it, grinning sheepishly. He explained he usually travels with his black carry-on and today he happened to use his wife's blue bag. He laughed it off and we exchanged fist bumps.

I congratulated him on "finding his bag" and off he went.

But 30 minutes prior, the last person he was willing to blame was himself. He kept insisting with increasing irritation somebody else must have moved his bag.

The point to the story is we're amazingly quick to blame everyone else. The last person we hold responsible tends to be ourselves. Entertaining the very chance we may actually be the culprits and made a mistake takes humility and professional maturity.

Next time you watch a sporting event whether it's basketball, football, baseball, soccer, or hockey, watch the players' reactions when they're called for a foul, a penalty, or a "called strike three." They reveal their character with every whistle blown.

Be Slow to Speak, Quick to Listen; and Slow to Anger

Some players own up to it right away, shaking their head "yep" or giving a "that was my bad" to their teammates and coaches. They take responsibility for their actions and mistakes. Other players immediately throw their hands up in the air in disbelief. They JUST. CAN'T. BELIEVE. A call was made against them? How dare the referee? How dare the umpire? How dare they? Filled with righteous indignation, it's as if they've never committed a foul, or never made illegal contact with a receiver more than five yards off the line of scrimmage. It's like they believe their own press and they're incapable of making a mistake.

The same thing goes for us at work and at home. Except it's not fouls or penalties we commit. In Chapter 11 I'll address the tendency we often have of trying to stretch a little too far beyond our role in the show. I call it Keep Your Passers Passin' and Your Shooters Shootin'. This means we end up less productive than we could be.

As a result, we sometimes forget to do something we promised we would do for others. We might knowingly break the rules. We leave out crucial parts of the story. We tell little white lies. Or, sometimes we don't mean it and we set out to crush it. We felt we crushed it; only to find out we weren't as awesome as we thought. Or, worst of all we run headlong into adversity. For example:

- We're not 100 percent in alignment with our boss.
- The one person at work who is always fighting us on issues gets the best of us again.
- One unfortunate circumstance after another piles up as if the deck is stacked against us.

Here's a quick secret: *You can't do this alone, and you're no match for this world by yourself.* I'm a redheaded, passionate guy who has a short fuse now and then. I'm learning and getting better at "managing my frustrations" but I still fall short. One verse in the Bible works perfectly for these awkward, annoying moments. In James 1:19 the good book says,

"Be slow to speak; quick to listen; and slow to anger."

Remember James 1:19, and reveal your character. You'll be glad you did because everyone else will marvel and appreciate your composed, professionally mature manner. Subsequently, the promotion you've been hoping for falls in your lap. The big sale finally comes through. Maybe, just maybe *those other people* who are so annoying become a little less so.

KEEP YOUR PASSERS PASSIN' AND YOUR SHOOTERS SHOOTIN'

CHAPTER 11

My Dad's basketball coach back in the 1970's had some great one-liners. I grew up with Dad telling me story after story about his favorite coach, Doc Murphy. His impersonation of Doc is awesome. If you know my Dad, or if you ever meet him, ask him to share a few "Doc-isms." Here are a few, but without my Dad's voice you don't get the full impact:

- The backboard's like the Bible, son, read it, learn it, know it!
- Boys, keep this one close, and I'll win it for ya.
- Second best, second best, second best, our *expletive, expletive* middle name is Second Best!
- A point guard that won't gamble ain't worth his or her salt
- "Very excellent…"
- Get it high and let it drop.
- Way to take 'em, babe!
- This would be a big feather in our cap!

They're better and funnier when brought to life with Dad's storytelling, but you get the point. Doc is still a charismatic character. There's one Doc-ism I always loved. After constantly hearing stories and coaching concepts growing up, this Doc-ism in particular is profoundly simple, but often missed, in both sports and business.

Doc would always say,

"Keep your passers passin' and your shooters shootin'."

How often have you seen a big fella stretching to do too much with the ball 30 or 40 feet away from the hoop in a basketball game? Sure, a few have the talent and that piece of their game dialed in, but that's the minority. Big fellas should stay underneath, in the paint, close to the basket. Makes sense, since they're taller than everyone else on the floor. The objective of the game is to get the orange, round ball in the hoop and score more points than the other team. So, it makes sense to keep the tallest players down low, on the block, not out along the three-point line trying to handle the ball or pass it off to a teammate. Usually it's a recipe for disaster because it's not what a scholar, professor, or especially a coach would call their "core competency."

Same concept goes for point guards who are great at handling the ball, directing traffic, and making great passes, as a facilitator for their team. Often those players aren't the greatest shooters. The reverse is also often true. Shooting guards are in that position because, well, they're great shooters. Often those players aren't the greatest ball-handlers, dribblers, or passers.

You get the point. It's best to "keep your passers, passing' and your shooters shootin'" so together the TEAM wins with everyone contributing the "specialty" they do best. Simply stay within your "core competency" and keep your team focused on what they do best.

Everyone Has "A" Role in the Show, Not "Every" Role in the Show

We see this all too often at work, in our jobs every day. Maybe it's a leader who thinks he or she knows the best marketing strategies and spends 75 percent of their time pontificating, lecturing, and driving marketing initiatives which should be handled by, um, the Marketing Team. Or, how about the staff member or peer you may be thinking of who always worries about what everyone else is doing or not doing and whether its correct or incorrect. He or she isn't the boss. They're probably not even a respected "leader among their peers." It would serve those folks well to focus on executing the role they were hired to do.

If you're a leader of people in any industry, you probably think this is a simple, no-brainer concept. On the surface, that's true. However, in the middle of the everyday grind, it's often overlooked. Think about your team, department, and even your entire organization. I haven't met you, nor do I know your current situation. But I bet you can point to at least a couple instances of people spending way too much time far removed from the tasks and functions for which they were hired in the first place.

Misalignment of employees' time not only costs companies money in wasted time, productivity, and efficiencies, it's also a root cause of burnout among the exact same teams that are out of alignment. How often do you experience seasons where it feels like you're working and working, spinning in circles yet making no progress? Too often. Usually you can connect the dots backwards and see along the way, one or two people may or may not have lost focus on their specific role in the show.

Find Out the Truth

So, attention all leaders and those who aspire to leadership: A FastPass to the levels of productivity and efficiency your company, your team or your executives are looking for is to absolutely make sure you have *the right people in the right roles*. Are you 100 percent certain you keep your passers passin' and your shooters shootin' all the time? If not, no problem. Call a quick timeout, roll up your sleeves, and determine "who's doing what" day-to-day.

make sure you have *the right people in the right roles*

Lee Cockerell, former Executive Vice President of Operations at *Walt Disney World* Resort® used to call it, "finding out the truth."

As a leader, people often tell you what they think you want to hear. Remember the stories you hear via email or in passing, going to and from meetings, may not be 100 percent accurate. Lee would encourage leaders, at every level, to get out and walk and talk with Cast Members, finding out the truth. That culture is still alive and well today, at Disney Parks and Resorts.

It's amazing what you discover when you stop, set aside an afternoon, morning, or even an hour, to talk with people. If you're doing it right, you're out engaging with your teams and each other anyway. While out and about, great leaders ask great questions. They're continually peeling the onion, getting under the layers and seeking to understand how people feel and most importantly what they're doing.

Step one is to engage, engage, engage with individuals and teams as often as possible. Then, assess the current landscape and identify the gaps between "what is" and "what should be." Once you make an assessment, move! Go.

Be the point guard or quarterback, and lean into your role as a leader or a leader among your peers. Ask the team to think how everyone is spending his or her time.

Make sure that:

- The Ops people are tightened up in their operational process execution;
- The Sales team is focused on sharing and selling the magic,
- The Finance team is dialed into counting every bean. God bless 'em. Every one.

Set the Table

As a leader of leaders in hotels for years, I had leaders who worked the opening shift bright and early. Then someone would come in and work the mid-shift covering the middle of the day. Finally, the beloved "closing shift" went until the wee hours of the following morning. For the opening shift, I would teach the team to "set the table" for the entire day. If the shop is set up well from the get-go, it sets the tone for the entire day. On the other hand, if we don't "set the table" getting the right people in the right roles at the right times of the day, we leave ourselves open for inefficiencies and missed opportunities which is not a winning recipe.

Setting the table appropriately with all the pieces, including people, process, and technology sets the tone for an entire organization or team of any size. Great teams have great individual contributors. Those individual contributions come from extremely talented people. When we don't have the place set up appropriately, with the right people in the right roles, we block our teams and especially those talented individuals from digging in and doing what they do best.

As leaders, we owe it to our talent to set them up well, allowing them to showcase how awesome they are at their job. We also owe it to our bosses and our organization to keep the right people in the right roles which insures we're being responsible stewards.

Who Will do What by When?

I'll end this chapter with how every leader should end a meeting, huddle, or conversation with the team. Once you have everyone in place, with the right people in the right roles, at the most appropriate times of the day and week, make sure everyone knows "who is doing what and by when."

Your teams will thank you. Talented high performers will thank you for keeping their efficiency and productivity levels where they want them and where you need them. The executives, board of directors or stockholders will thank you for the profitability.

All will be well, when you keep your passers passin' and your shooters shootin'. Thank you, Coach Doc Murphy, for this timeless, transferrable pearl of wisdom.

PART THREE

PLAY
(WORK)
HARD

HUSTLE – OUTWORK, OUTSMART, AND OUT-AWESOME EVERYONE

CHAPTER 12

What's the scariest thing to any competitor in sports, business, entrepreneurship, or any other competitive environment? Is it the fear of losing? Maybe. The thought of someone else out there working harder, getting smarter and more prepared than you can strike fear into the heart of a competitor. Any rival worth his or her salt, wants to "win" and hates to lose. Yet knowing someone else is working harder, "wanting it" more and "earning it" more, whatever "it" may be, is even scarier than losing or coming up short of the goal.

There Are No Shortcuts

Remember Hoop Stars Basketball Camp I told you about? Early that week, I was in a scrimmage against the players a year older than me. These were Kentucky All-Stars I'd read about in the newspaper, with impressive statistics, cool guy quotes to their local sports reporters and pictures of them suspended in air dunking on people. During this scrimmage, I was in good form, playing well. I was a nervous wreck, but made some shots early and a few good passes, so I was feelin' the magic. After my pep talk from Coach Baker, I truly "believed I belonged."

There was a loose ball on the floor, and I was the closest player, so I hopped over to grab it when out of the blue appeared six feet four inches of pure Kentucky High School Basketball greatness. I even remember his name, Ryan Steger. He was on the "other team" and he came diving toward me. Before I knew it, he dove on the floor, beat me to the ball and flipped it to one of his teammates. His teammate took two dribbles, right to their basket, dunking it with authority while hanging on the rim and smacking the glass on his way back to Earth.

Ryan's collision knocked me off the court and basically into the bleachers. I rolled over and looked up at one of the coaches as if to say, "Come on! How 'bout a foul!?"

He peered down at me. I remember the moment like it was yesterday. He simply said, with a shoulder shrug, "…Hey man, he just wanted it more."

Gross.

No way did he want it more. Are you kidding me? I just had a breakthrough lesson from Coach Baker. I was beginning to believe I belonged right out there with them, playing with the best. The worst part, I was hot. So, no way did he want it more, I thought to myself. But wait, he sacrificed. Steger threw caution to the wind with his all-out dive to the floor. He flat out beat me to the ball and out-hustled me. Maybe in that moment, he did want it more than me.

Was that play the end of the world? No, absolutely not. It just didn't feel great, knowing I was out-hustled. It didn't feel great and it certainly didn't help my team. Plus, it certainly didn't help my case to prove to myself and everyone else "I belonged" out there with the All-Stars.

This is one of those principles we heard from our coaches, which absolutely applies to everyone's job today, regardless of your business or industry. There are no shortcuts, plain and simple. Being great or even successful takes hard work, especially if you intend to reach your own or your organization's goals and objectives. Nothing is easy. In fact, anything worth doing is hard, which is why they call it "work."

What does "hustle" look like where you work? Everyone's job is different, but if you put your mind to it I'll bet you can find some commonalities in terms of how everyone can out hustle the competition. Remember, successful people consistently do things unsuccessful people refuse to do with any consistency. So, out-hustling others may not be as bad or as hard as you think to land the job or beat out that competitor for the business.

> *Remember, successful people consistently do things unsuccessful people refuse to do with any consistency.*

Playing to Win Instead of Playing "Not to Lose"

Too often we see sports teams playing well, jumping out to a huge lead, only to lose the lead and the game in the end. Why? They got satisfied and too comfortable. Ever seen it before? Teams are aggressive early, playing with gusto, taking chances, trying new things, and making them work. They're executing and winning. Then, they try and "protect their lead" and coast on in, hoping the other team doesn't score enough to take the lead and beat them. That's playing not to lose instead of playing to win. Plus, "hope" is never a winning strategy.

Annoying.

Playing not to lose can happen in our careers, too. We're young, new, and full of fresh, bright ideas and boundless energy. You attack your job, diving after the "loose balls," staying late, coming in early, collaborating, finding solutions, and you flat out get it done. Then, you get the promotion or a couple accolades. In some cases, you even gain positive street cred among the bosses. Suddenly, it's easy to be cautious and conservative, because you don't want to lose all the respect, admiration, and credibility you worked so hard to gain. I see it all the time and I've caught myself sliding into this trap as well.

Don't fall into it. When you stop getting after it, with that same gusto you know you're capable of, count on someone else, a coworker or the competition, to appear out of nowhere and knock you into the bleachers as they snatch the glory from your hands in a heartbeat. Come on, no way do they want it more than you. There's no way they're smarter than you. No way will they out work you. Don't let them. Don't give in to the voices in your head telling you to hang back a bit and play it safe. Keep hustling.

Remember, your hustle and gusto got you this far, through adversity and into this position. So, stay around the ball, a concept we'll unpack in Chapter 13. It's all about staying laser-focused, and involved in what matters the most in your company or organization. Keep seeking to understand, and for sure keep adding your two cents. Real leaders, the ones you'll want to work for and align with in the long run, will notice you're a person who plays to win, as opposed to playing not to lose. Trust me, you'll always be in demand. When you play to win, by consistently adding value to those around you, you'll make yourself indispensable. That's a rare quality, which will earn you the ball every single time.

Snap to Whistle

In football, coaches call on their teams to go "snap to whistle" on every play. That means they want a 100 percent effort from the time the ball is snapped, all the way until the whistle blows to end the play.

An easy way to out-hustle others at work is to go "snap to whistle" every single workday. Jeepers, creepers. Nothing is more annoying, as a leader of people, than when people on your team sashay into work late and always ask to leave early. Sometimes they don't even ask and just slip out when they think you're not looking. Equally annoying is having your own peers or worse, your leader, show up late and leave early consistently; especially when you're putting in the productive hours, the heart, soul, blood, sweat, and tears to move the team forward.

Yes, it's frustrating, but it's also an opportunity. The reality is most of the people where you work lackadaisically show up either on time or even a smidge late. More importantly, while everyone is supposedly "working," how often are 100 percent of the people actually working 100 percent of the time. Basically, never.

What if you showed up 30 minutes early and stayed 30 minutes later than everyone else in your office or your competitor's office? That's an extra hour per day, times 20 days per month, assuming you work five days per week for four weeks per month. So, you'd put in 20 additional hours per month, times 12 months per year, which comes out to working 240 more hours per year, roughly an extra six weeks more per year than anyone else.

Wait. It gets even better.

Consider the realities of your situation while everyone is at work at the same time. Think about all the slackers around you. They think they want it, but they're slackers. Let's assume you hustle, every day. While the average person is at the water cooler, in the break room or taking a two-hour lunch, you're working and hustling. So, you're potentially working two hours more per day than the average slacker. You could conceivably be working an extra two hours per day more than "average people."

Dude, that's an extra ten hours per week, an extra 40 hours per month, and an extra 480 hours per year more than "the other guy or girl" is working. That's the equivalent of an additional 12 workweeks per year. It's a no-brainer. You have to achieve way more than everyone else when you're putting the pedal to the metal every single day.

A little hustle here, and a little hustle there, adds up over time. Suffice it to say, you can certainly get out far ahead of the masses, master your craft, out work, out smart, and out hustle everyone by working 12 more weeks per year than them.

You just have to want it more. I think you do. Hustle.

BE AROUND THE BALL – BECOME NOTICED AND KNOWN

CHAPTER 13

Shoes squeaking, popcorn popping, and fans yelling. I remember it almost like yesterday. I was sitting in the bleachers, watching a high school basketball game with my Dad. My high school basketball coach, Charles Baker was there, too. I was the starting point guard on our school team, but we were off that evening; so, we drove a few towns away to watch some Kentucky high school basketball action. As long as I can remember, one of my favorite things was and still is attending live sporting events and escaping reality for a couple hours. The conversations we shared during the game, especially with my Dad and Coach Baker, always added to the experience. We'd break down the defensive strategies, offensive plays, missed calls, and everything else in between.

It was a few days after Christmas at a well-loved annual holiday tournament near my hometown. The joint was packed with spectators in their winter jackets, hats and scarves. That unique sporting event energy and enthusiasm filled the gymnasium. As the referee's whistle blew, the ball was tipped and the game began. Is there anything better than sports?

Extraordinarily Talented People are Involved in Every Play

I remember one particular player. He was a few notches above anyone else playing on the floor that night. I was impressed. So impressed I commented to Coach Baker, "Coach, that guy's good!" I shouted above the band playing, the cheerleaders cheering and the stomping feet pounding the wooden bleachers with a deafening roar.

Little did I know his response that night would ring in my head for the next 20 years. Another valuable nugget I learned from my experiences in sports, which applies brilliantly at work in a professional setting. Coach said, "Yes, Taylor, he's a very nice player, he's always around the ball."

As I thought about what he said, I watched the kid play more closely. On offense or on defense, whether he was the team member shooting and scoring or scrambling to guard the other guy with the ball, he was always, literally *around the ball*. If a shot went up, he was either the guy rebounding the miss, or at a minimum he was constantly where the action was taking place.

Coach was absolutely right. Great players in sports and in life always seek out valuable ways to be involved in every play. On occasion, they take the shot, other times they make a great pass to set-up a teammate for an easy score. Sometimes they make a crucial defensive play which turns the tide of the whole game. The common denominator among all of them? They're always "around the ball" making an impact for their team.

The same concept can be applied to your daily routine at work.

You're all buttoned up. Your desk is tidy and neat. Your To-Do list is quite a masterpiece with your yellow highlighter drawn through each item. But where's the ball? What are the most vital initiatives in your company, organization, team or school? Or, are you focused on something far away from "the ball" as I suggested a few pages back in Chapter 11? How about for your own family at home?

- Are you enthusiastically involved all the time?

- Are you making an impact that makes a difference?
- Or, are you satisfied merely having your own projects wrapped up?

Do you want to do more, achieve more and make a positive difference to your overall team, organization, family and relationships? If you want to be an influential game changer and make a powerful impact; once your personal to-dos are crossed off your list, go OneMoreStep. Seek out ways to participate in your organization's most pressing projects or most important objectives.

You say it's not in your job description, but you know you can add value? Get in there. Don't wait to be asked. Jump right in, and create some magic.

Magic Happens in the Middle, Not the Sidelines

A great NBA and NCAA head basketball coach once said about point guards, "Mediocre guards play along the sidelines, but great guards always can be found playing in the middle of the court." Next time you watch a sporting event, watch it differently. Chances are you already watch the action on the floor or out on the field. This time, watch the risks being taken and the potential game-changing plays happening in center court. Along the sidelines far less is happening. It's easier and less risky. Good luck making any "real magic" or a positive impact while hanging out, hugging the sidelines.

Get in the middle of the floor or field, metaphorically speaking. When you think the "big project" or initiative coming down from the CEO, owners, or the corporate office is over your head and unrelated to your job title, go OneMoreStep. Seek out valuable ways to get in the mix, and make it happen. Do it a few times soon. You'll become known and recognized as someone who tends to always be around the ball. Then, allow me to be the first person to congratulate you on your next promotion.

Be around the ball at work and in your life as much as you can. If you know you can contribute in a positive way, why not ask to get involved? Ask to be the one who takes that last second shot. You know you want the ball, in crucial situations at work. So staying *around the ball* consistently will absolutely *earn you the ball* sooner vs. later. That could be the essential OneMoreStep your company, team or school needs to go over the top and be successful.

Remove "That's Not My Job" From Your Vocabulary

In late-2010 during our pre-opening season, one of our Vice Presidents at the Cosmopolitan of Las Vegas was tasked with overseeing day-to-day operations of one department in the casino known as Slot Operations. However, on any given day of the week, he could be found in a meeting with the marketing or accounting teams, making decisions that impacted Guest Experience at the front desk, answering questions for hotel guests or employees on the casino floor or assisting with the planning of special events. If something important was happening, needed to be approved, or if someone needed assistance, he was usually there ready and happy to help. He made it his business to constantly be around the ball.

Somewhere, buried in the Human Resources department, there was a job description for his role. But he always went above and beyond. He went to work every day to make a difference. Period. Not once did I hear the words "that's not my job" come out of his mouth. He was a leader among his peers, always representing his "nation" well. It never would've stopped him from contributing anyway. He was concerned with the big picture; the team; the company. That's leadership and taking ownership. That's going OneMoreStep and it stands out in a big way.

We all want to *stand out*. Deep down inside, each one of us wants to be recognized or known for something. I'm guessing you're no different. In the context of your everyday grind, the one you begrudgingly drag yourself to day in and day out, there are ways to

We all want to stand out. Deep down inside, each one of us wants to be recognized or known for something.

stand out and make a difference. The place you call work; the daily grind with the slackers, the micro-managing boss who never bothers to listen. Yep, the one with the suffocating corporate… "corporateness." I just made up a new word. Go with it. It may catch on. I believe there are always numerous ways to distinguish yourself by being around the ball.

While in the daily grind, feeling like a hamster in a wheel, choosing to be around the ball not only gets you out of the mind-numbing sameness, it also sets you apart. Just like that extraordinary player I noticed one Kentucky High School basketball night watching the game with my Dad and Coach Baker. He was amazing. When you choose to stand out today at work you can completely change the game not only for yourself and your own sanity, but for your team members as well.

Mark Sanborn, speaker and best-selling author of The Fred Factor teaches us, "The best job skill of the past 1,000 years will be the best job skill of the next 1,000 years and that's the ability to create value for others."

Try it today or this week, at work, at home, or in your community. Don't be shy or hang back. If or when you feel you've got all your ducks in a row and you're feeling all tidied up with your work, look around and listen:

- Where's "the ball" where you work right now?
- What are the mission critical projects, initiatives, or hot buttons?
- Where's the ball in your family or personal relationships?

Dive into the action and be around the ball today. Don't put it off. You'll change the game for your coworkers, your team, and maybe even your boss.

Let me share a quick secret: Changing the game positively for your boss is a good thing. Being noticed by others in your organization, especially your boss, isn't even the best part. The best part is the feeling of knowing you made an impact and a difference that truly matters.

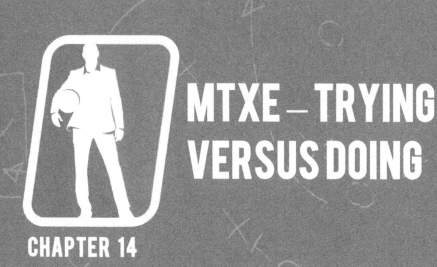

MTXE – TRYING VERSUS DOING

CHAPTER 14

You may have noticed; basketball season is my favorite season and basketball is my favorite sport. Personally, I believe March Madness should be a nationally recognized holiday. Why? Because it serves as the long-awaited, electrifying crescendo to high school and college basketball players' and fans' seasons. There should be no work and no school. It should be like the holidays. Bars and restaurants should be open all day and night, and every person in the world should pause and immerse themselves in pure, holy basketball bliss.

As we're discussing the threads between sports and our everyday lives at work and at home, I can't help but reflect on my glory days as a high school basketball player in Eastern Kentucky. I grew up in Carter County and played for the East Carter Raiders. My fellow alumni from East Carter High School grew up with a slogan, a tag line, our own motto, if you will. It's MTXE.

MTXE stands for
Mental Toughness, Extra Effort

Growing up falling in love with basketball, I looked up to my Dad, my coaches, and the East Carter Raiders who played before me. MTXE was a concept that always gave me hope, fired me up and, kept me believing in both myself and others. I still believe *anything is possible* with a little mental toughness and extra effort.

anything is possible with a little mental toughness and extra effort.

Get the Job Done

I remember as a sophomore in high school I was a starter on the Junior Varsity team. One time I came off the bench for several minutes in the 7:00 pm Varsity game. In a home game, Coach Baker back-pedaled down the sideline, reached for me and put me in the game. Minutes later I found myself in the throes of Varsity action, with a million things happening all at once. A teammate knocked the ball away from the opposing team. I was close to it, but didn't run it down fast enough. The ball trickled out of bounds. Since it was last touched by the Raiders, the ball went to the other team.

As luck would have it, this all happened directly in front of our own bench. Coach Baker gave me a bit of a motivational speech, to put it mildly, and offered his, well, *coaching*. He told me, "Get after it! Come up with those loose balls."

I replied, "I tried."

Bad move on my part. Coach quickly took advantage of a teachable/coachable moment and offered his *coaching* again. He barked out, "Trying won't cut it. Get the job done!"

From that moment on in basketball and in life I've always wanted to get the job done. Perhaps, in part I was scarred for life after being coached in front of a gymnasium full of people, in front of my teammates, directly in front of our own bench.

Some days are better than others. Some things are easier to accomplish than others. There are days when the loose balls on the floor are easily scooped up, while other times we miss it. We miss the ball, miss our chance, and miss our opportunity.

But in life, just like in basketball you can always get the ball back. You can always get the job done with a little MTXE, Mental Toughness Extra Effort.

There are moments when you're all buttoned up and have a fundamental understanding of everything that needs to happen. You're mentally prepared, yet you slow down and lose steam halfway through a project, a semester, an event, an endeavor, or a career once adversity and challenging moments set in. That's "trying" at its finest.

Next time adversity sets in, with a million things happening at once, think MTXE.

Dig in, take a deep breath and get mentally tough. You're smart enough. You and your team can do it. Be the "thought leader" who goes OneMoreStep and rallies the team to pause, take a deep breath, and a more cerebral approach. And then…

Then, go another step with the *extra effort*. It's all about the extra five minutes you take to teach someone something. Whether it's extra emails to clarify instructions, extra time listening to someone else's concerns. Or, an extra hour or two of your own effort, staying 100 percent devoted to your cause. MTXE creates the OneMoreStep that can make a big difference to you, your peers, your friends and the ones you love.

Are you *trying* or are you *doing*?

Go OneMoreStep and think MTXE – Mental Toughness Extra Effort. I promise more often than not, you'll get the job done. Whatever you do, never tell a boss, a leader, or even a teammate, "I'm trying."

Don't ever make the same lame mistake I made with Coach Baker back in that game. Just say, "I'll get it done, Boss."

Chances are, they hear "I'm trying" from others all day long. Be the one person who changes the narrative and changes the game. You'll clearly become the one person who can always be counted on to "get the job done."

One for the road… on Leap Day, February 29th, 1996…

62nd District Tournament: East Carter Raiders vs. Lewis County Lions

Our team, the Raiders, had only won seven games up to that point in the entire season. Lewis County was definitely a better team, with great players. The game site was on Lewis County's home floor with their fans. We were outmatched and we knew it. By all accounts, projections, and forecasts the Raiders were obviously going to lose.

The game went back and forth; it was nip and tuck throughout. Long story short, I hit a layup with time running down in regulation to force overtime. I was also lucky enough to hit a 3-pointer with barely a second on the clock at the end of the first overtime to ultimately tie the game, forcing a second overtime.

We won that game when all the odds were against us in double overtime. We won on the opposing team's home court. A week prior, everyone from players to fans to sports reporters to the custodial staff thought there was no possible way the East Carter Raiders could ever beat the Lewis County Lions.

I don't share the above game "stats" to brag about how awesome I am or was, although it certainly was one shining moment. I highlight this game and experience because we won it with Mental Toughness and Extra Effort.

Our coaches in sports had a game plan and they taught us. No matter what sport we played back in school they coached us, encouraged us, and showed us what it means to be mentally tough. They motivated and inspired us to put forth the *extra effort* whether it was in basketball, soccer, field hockey, swimming, track, football or another sport.

Finally, that extra effort against the Lewis County Lions allowed us to withstand a grueling game with not one but two overtimes. In the end, we came out victorious.

Thanks to Coach Baker, Coach "E", Coach Calhoun, and Doc Bender for teaching me then and for inspiring me now. Over 20 years later I still live, breathe, walk, and talk – MTXE.

The operative word here is doing. Not trying. Doing.

If you're honest, as you think about the people you live with and work with, every day, including your loved ones, some of them are mentally tough. Others may work incredibly hard. But how many people, including yourself, do you know who actually combine both those qualities all the time? To be both *mentally tough* and put in the *extra effort* is rare. It's special. That's why it's worth doing consistently, every day. The operative word here is *doing*. Not trying. Doing.

Doing = SMART Goals, Tactical Game Plans, and Old Fashioned Execution

Most of us have encountered the inquiring minds of leaders, executives, or bosses, asking about substandard performances or results. While dreadfully annoying, it's their job to ask such questions. After they ask, "what happened", their next question is usually, "what are you doing about it?" In Chapter 15 we'll address the importance of having good conversations, early and often, which help with this dynamic.

A great way to be prepared for these inevitable calls or emails from above is to simply have your goals and tactical game plans tightly and thoughtfully constructed before they even ask you the question. Once goals and tactical game plans are created and aligned to righting the ship of your organization, that's when the MTXE comes into play with old-fashioned execution. Day in and day out, simply executing yours or your organization's game plan with focus and urgency is not only the quickest way to keep annoying bosses off your back, it's also the best way to insure you're constantly "doing" as opposed to merely "trying."

Take the time to come up with your own SMART goals for yourself or your team. These are goals, which are specific, measurable, attainable, relevant, and time specific. Be thoughtful and intentional about how you'll spend your time. Talk about it to the people who support and encourage you. Write it all down in a game plan, the same way a coach, or a professional athlete defines his or her path to success. Then, wake up every single day, and execute.

That's how you crush it. One day at a time. Doing versus merely trying. Before you know it, your boss will stop asking you what you're doing, and he or she will start asking you to share your value-added goals and tactical game plans with others in the organization. And, boom. You're labeled as a "doer" in the eyes of your peers and leaders. That bodes well for your future.

I'll sum up this chapter with a simple quote from one of the greatest coaches of all time, Yoda, who in The Empire Strikes Back famously said, "Do or do not. There is no try."

CONVERSATIONS MAKE GOOD COMPANY

CHAPTER 15

In the 2016 NBA season, the Cleveland Cavaliers found themselves primed and ready for greatness. With solid role players to complement the big three superstars: Lebron James, Kevin Love, and Kyrie Irving, the Cavs had the gift of talent to be great.

However, their season wasn't without obstacles and bumps along the way. The reality TV show that is the Twitterverse and social media kept us entertained with what seemed like an ongoing soap opera among the big three superstars.

Did Lebron call out Kyrie? Did Kevin Love get his feelings hurt? Do the Cavs have dissension among the ranks in King James' court? It was literally like a real life show, "only on Bravo" rather than ESPN.

Breakthroughs Happen with Conversation

Then, a breakthrough happened. I remember watching Sports Center, and seeing an interview with the big three. Lebron, K. Love and Kyrie talked about how they all now "understand each other better." They referenced a breakthrough meeting between the three of them behind closed doors, in which they simply had a conversation. They talked about how they all suddenly knew what each guy wanted individually and how each of their contributions could and would help the team win.

They went on to win the 2016 NBA Championship in dramatic, storybook fashion.

Whether it's the company we keep or the companies for whom we work, the quality conversations we have are what make them good.

Some businesses and organizations are well-oiled machines with a well-known brand name to go with it. Others fight, scratch, and claw their way through the tedious day-to-day, just to make ends meet for their Guests, Clients, Customers, Staff, and other key stakeholders.

What truly makes a business "good?" Is it the brand, its fancy buildings, impressive balance sheet, or ranking on a recent Forbes list? Maybe. Those things certainly don't hurt.

Engagement Makes the Difference that Matters

Companies can be number one on everything from Forbes List XYZ to the stock market ticker. However, all it takes is one person to ruin the perception or reputation. In the same way, small businesses up and down Main Street USA without the same level of financing, infrastructure, or resources we often find in corporate America can create and deliver fantastic experiences for their Guests, Customers and Clients as long as engagement with people is memorable, in a good way.

So, while it's nice to have corporate infrastructure and the power of "the brand," the real power that fuels the engine of any company is good, old-fashioned conversation. In fact, in a day when you're completely over it – it just may be the MTXE and hustle that changes the narrative.

That's great news for any person, anywhere, working for any business or organization on the planet. This includes you and me. Whatever your role, in whatever company, big or small, you have an opportunity to:

- Inspire others or be inspired
- Change your perception or their perception
- Raise the level of satisfaction by doing the work

All it takes is talking with other people. Engage in conversation with a genuine interest in what you can learn from others, or, make an honest effort to help others. This can be the difference between being upset with someone and creating a meaningful relationship. It's true for the company that employs you as well as the company that surrounds you. Conversations make good company.

So, what factors make conversations "good?"

Worthwhile Content

Like anything else, the content of a conversation will provide the substance you remember. Just like in the online, ecommerce space, top experts will say for any Internet company to be successful, they must understand the golden rule: Content is King.

Online gurus tell us the following attributes make online content great:

- Relevant, compelling information
- Visitor/User Friendliness
- Quality Control
- Something others would recommend
- Supplies the searcher's needs

A perfect illustration of these five factors is Amazon.com. Consider why so many of us go back time and again to their site to buy things:

- Dynamic content, completely customizing the experience for you as you shop or surf with "related items" and "recommended items." They make it all about you.

- Their content offers reminders that comfort us, like the strike-through of the Manufacturer's Suggested Retail Price and the lower Amazon.com price. Customer Reviews and the "Look Inside" feature for books suggest even more "why's." Amazon tells us *why we should buy from them.*
- They use a *pull rather than push approach.* Their content reminds us multiple times, "You can review this order before it's final." It's as if they're reassuring you, "We're not forcing you to do anything." That makes Amazon customers comfortable, keeps them engaged, and results in increased revenues.

You can take these same online principles and apply them to the content of your conversations. Whether you're a manager, doctor, lawyer, schoolteacher, sales person, leader, coach, teammate, friend, and/or loving family member, you have your own "content" as does everyone else. Then, content gets "published" by way of the conversations you have with others including the:

- Emails you send your teams and leaders in the organization,
- Lessons you prepare for and ultimately deliver.
- Services you provide to your Guests, and the
- Proposals you pitch to your prospective clients.

Ask yourself if your "content" makes it relevant to *them.* Do you make it easy or difficult for people to work with you? Do you save *them* time and make it convenient? Is your work or your leadership something *they* would recommend to others? Do you dynamically cater to others' needs, making it about them? Do you give *them* the "why's" behind the decisions you make or your views? Do you meet *them* where *they* are and pull rather than push?

Environment and Context

Frequently conversations leave us feeling more confused than clear, more upset than at ease, and more frustrated with the other person.

Why is this? Too often we simply don't know where the other person's coming from on certain topics of conversation. Maybe they don't understand where our sudden burst of conviction and passion is coming from on those exact same topics. Perhaps it doesn't seem relevant to them. They and we, far too often, just don't know why.

So, why not tell 'em why? Give people the why's for your passion. Give them the context, the reason, the back-story, and the challenges. Give them the CONTEXT of the situation. The OneMoreStep lies in not only providing the context, but when the situation is reversed, ASKING FOR the context.

It's easy to preach, pontificate, and dictate your thoughts and convictions. That's what everyone usually does; which generally turns off most people:

- On the other end of the phone,
- In the other department, or,
- Those with a completely opposite point of view.

As a result, relationships go nowhere fast.

On the other hand, when you pause, take a deep breath, and ask for more context, great progress happens. If and when you not only ask, but listen to their reply as well, that's when understanding begins. That's also when they begin feeling more comfortable with you. That comfort level gradually leads to TRUST, and trust is the only thing that leads to thriving, productive relationships.

The challenge of taking the time to discover another person's perspective and their "why" is usually rooted in an inability to communicate effectively. The missing link is often context.

Context is important. Provide it and ask for it.

Clear Expectations

The difference between expectations and reality often leaves us with an array of emotions, ranging from stress, anxiety, anger, fear, sadness and disappointment. Not the least of these is misery.

Most of us can agree we'd rather not be miserable. You'd rather not live under the burden of undue stress, anxiety, anger, fear, sadness, and/or disappointment. So, it stands to reason most of the people you work with or live with feel the same.

Taking the time to improve conversational skills is one of the little things, which can make a big impact.

Providing clear expectations when you talk with people can prevent unnecessary pressure and anxiety from creeping into their already stressful day. It's one of the "little things" I'll unpack in Chapter 16. A conversation may not seem like a big deal, but it is when you consider the negative impact of people feeling like they're not heard or understood. Taking the time to improve conversational skills is one of the little things, which can make a big impact.

You actually have the ability and the power to protect people from feeling miserable and that's a big deal. So, if you put your mind to it, you have the opportunity to reduce misery in the world. You can start by giving and asking for clear expectations, one conversation at a time.

Be aware of and intentional about the content you provide in conversations. Ask for and provide context and clear expectations. You'll be pleasantly surprised how the overwhelmingly maddening day-to-day grind can easily be transformed into something more fun and meaningful.

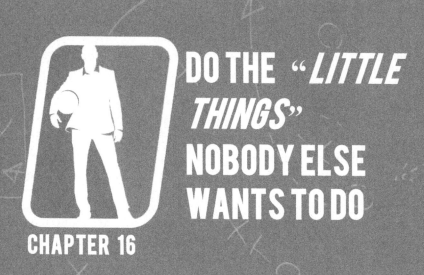

DO THE "*LITTLE THINGS*" NOBODY ELSE WANTS TO DO

CHAPTER 16

Ever wonder if your boss, friends, family, or your coworkers understand how much honest effort you put into things? Does it ever seem like you constantly work and work and work… and stress and stress and stress to do your very best? For what? Do people really care?

Consider the following.

Never Underestimate Your Impact

What if you stopped doing all those little things? Consider the negative impact a general lack of effort or caring would have on your bosses, friends, family, coworkers, etc. The truth is sometimes the things we think are the most menial and random of tasks; truly mean the most to other people. Yet we never truly understand how much we impact them. So, I suggest you keep doing the little things, which truly do add up, even if it doesn't always feel like it.

If you're a salesperson, keep taking that extra thirty minutes to think about how to ask the right questions in the right way of your clients and prospects. Surprisingly, that little thing just might make the difference in closing the business or losing the business.

If you're a schoolteacher, keep going in early to brush up your lesson plans for the day. Your extra attention to detail might be the secret sauce which leads to a magical "breakthrough moment" for a student who's been struggling.

If you're an event planner, keep going in on your days off for those one to three hours to make sure an event goes off without a hitch. That extra little step might be the reason you're able to make someone's party, event, or meeting one of the most thrilling and memorable days of their life.

Once again, it's about mastering and perfecting the fundamentals we tackled in Chapter 8. If you lead a team, keep spending quality time with each individual team member. Keep asking them:

- What are they enjoying about their experience at work?
- What would they like to change?
- And, how can you help them achieve their next goal?

Those conversations with you might be what keeps them getting out of bed each morning to come to work. Your time spent walking and talking with them may seem menial to you, but it could mean the world to them.

If you're currently between jobs now, keep sending those hand-written thank you cards to companies that granted you an interview. Keep praying. Keep serving. Keep getting after it every day. Your positive attitude will ultimately be what somebody, somewhere sees in you, which will eventually lead to those magical words, "You're hired." I've been unemployed twice since 2008. So yes, I get it. Just keep going OneMoreStep. Keep doing the little things.

Successful people always do the things unsuccessful people won't bother to do.

Trust the process. Successful people always do the things unsuccessful people won't bother to do. Take a break for ten minutes here or there. But remember, keep believing you belong, and keep doing the right thing.

The Grind

In my mid-thirties, I led a team of sales people at Disney Vacation Club. (*Disney Vacation Club is Disney's version of "vacation ownership." Guests have the opportunity to purchase a deeded real estate interest in one of the Disney Vacation Club Resorts.*) In many ways, the product sells itself. But the *process* and *grind* of it can get as tedious as any other role in Sales or any other business function, for that matter.

As talented and charismatic as you might imagine teams of professionals are at Disney, they still must practice. Reminding successful, entrepreneurial 25-year real estate sales professionals that he or she might need practice was one of the most awkward and challenging aspects of my role. I think I know how Coach Phil Jackson felt years ago, when he coached Michael Jordan and Scottie Pippen. Later in his career he coached Kobe Bryant and Shaquille O'Neal. More of the same sentiment.

About 20 months into my new job as a Manager of Sales at DVC, I realized people would never be as successful as they could be in their jobs unless they practiced and mastered the process. So, I began holding a weekly one-hour review session with the team, doing drills and exercises, allowing them time to practice their trade, their presentation which they delivered daily to Guests and Leads. It's no different than a basketball player putting in the time on shooting or dribbling drills, a pro golfer hitting bucket after bucket of balls on the driving range, or a baseball player carving out ample time each week for batting practice. Professional sales people should constantly practice their trade just like any other professional, athlete or otherwise.

Some folks on the DVC team loved it, and looked forward to it each week. Others actually came in on their days off for the sessions. As you may expect, not everyone loved to practice. In fact, several of them, each week, thought they had better, more important things to do. I always felt like Coach Jimmy Dugan, Tom Hanks' character in the movie *A League of Their Own*, when he's herding the team of women ballplayers out of the house into the caravan to get to the ballpark early for batting practice. Jimmy says, "…Alright let's go. Gotta get there for batting practice. And if you don't think you need it, *think again! Think again!"*

But I digress…

There's no doubt it was tedious. It was a bit of a grind to "herd the cats," preparing what amounted to lesson plans for each week. The purpose was to give us a weekly roadmap for training and practice. One day I was reminded just how important the *little things* like "lesson plans" and practice sessions were to my team when a guy on the team popped into my office.

Salespeople, God bless 'em, have no problem mastering the art of the "pop-in" visit. They charismatically drop in, whether you're on an important call, typing an email to an executive, or even just trying to think. Their greatest skill is "The Pop-In" as they typically break my train of thought and interrupt while making me laugh at the same time. So, I forget how annoying they're about to be a moment before I'm annoyed. If your work is anything like mine, the next thing you know, you're irritated but not really because the moment is gone. Plus, they left you on such a high note – they were smiling, you were smiling. But then…wait…what? You lost your train of thought. See, I just did it to you. What were we talking about? Squirrel.

Oh, yeah. It was about quitting time on Saturday night, which was my Friday night because I was off on Sundays and Mondays. A newer Cast member on the team *popped into* my office. He said, "Hey boss…that family just joined! And, I've had two other sales in the past two days. It's all because of that *practice session* we had last Thursday!"

I'm a rather sensitive guy, and mostly love teaching and coaching. But let's face it; teaching, coaching and any other job can get tedious after a while. The consistency we've already mentioned adds value and it's one factor that keeps us fighting through the tediousness.

He continued, "Thursday morning, before the meeting, I was gonna come talk to you about everything. I was freaking out, not sure if this job will work out for me. But I want you to know I got all three of these sales because of the *practice* we've been doing; especially that session on Thursday."

When you play golf and suck – you're slicing and hooking all over and your last drive off the tee is perfect, it brings you out to play golf another day. Let's be honest, sometimes you have to keep fighting through it all. I'll explain more about it in the next chapter. That's what this felt like. After the grind of yet another week coming to a close, with self doubt creeping in, I got the "feedback equivalent" of lacing a drive 225 yards down the middle of the fairway off the 18th tee box after an afternoon of frustrating golf shots. It keeps you coming back the next time.

I got choked up, and almost teared up. But I played it off like my eyes were watering. Exhausted, I just smiled. I told him how proud I was of him, congratulated him, and reminded him, "You got the stuff. That's why I picked you."

One of my high performers, another great guy and absolute professional sales person, overheard the conversation, and *popped over*, looking over his teammate's shoulder at me. He was far more seasoned and quite the successful professional with whom I often exchanged ideas, strategies, and feedback. He just winked and smiled which said it all. It told me to *keep doing the little things*.

We never know how our work touches people. Trust that you're making an impact. Especially when you doubt it, and especially when it gets tedious. Focus on the "work that matters" not the dumb job. If it feels tedious, it means you're doing something few others would bother taking the time and effort to do. That alone adds value and sets you apart from the pack. Keep *doing what you're doing*. Because if you stop, people lose out on your small but powerful, daily dose of magic, which just could be the thing that keeps them going. It could also be that very "little thing" which continues to make you stand out.

FIGHT THROUGH IT – FOURTH QUARTER – FINISH STRONG

CHAPTER 17

Bottom of the eighth on a balmy November evening, the Chicago Cubs had blown a 6-3 lead over the Cleveland Indians. It was game seven. Game seven! In a game that had everything from rain delays to extra innings the Cubs did something they hadn't done in 108 seasons. They dug deep, rallied and won the 2016 World Series in the tenth inning.

During high school football games, at the end of the third quarter, the whistle would blow. It was a signal. Every player on the field, the sidelines, every cheerleader, every fan in the stadium, and all in East Carter Raider Nation would hold up four fingers. Every person threw four fingers up high above their head to indicate it was now the FOURTH QUARTER. As if we all said in unison, "We're not giving up, we're not losing faith. We're giving it our all. As long as there's time on the clock, we'll finish strong, in the fourth quarter!"

Toward the end of each basketball practice, while putting us through extensive drills and/or strength and conditioning workouts, coaches would shout, "FOURTH QUARTER!" I didn't know it back then but it was as if they were preparing us for real life situations. Those two words said, "I know you're tired. I know it's been a long day, a long practice, and a long three quarters. But there's still time on the clock, and the fourth quarter just might be where we make our move. That's when everyone else gives up and submits to their weaknesses. If we can dig deep, reach down, stick together, and go OneMoreStep mentally and physically; this could be our time to make our move in the fourth quarter."

It's Up to You

For you and I, today could be our moment. This could be your time.

No matter how rough, or challenging your year, month, week or even your day has been so far, you and I have the opportunity to make a real difference. We can make a very positive difference at any time, any day. All you have to do is make a choice and decide to do it.

If it's been rough at work, and you think it's a lost cause to keep putting forth so much effort, think again and think differently. Keep being the best version of you, because you never know who's in the background watching, who's listening, and who's secretly loving, appreciating, and valuing all your efforts.

Feeling discouraged? For so long now you've dreamed of that next opportunity, the ideal girl, the perfect guy, the dream life you've always wanted. Has this year fallen way short of your goals and expectations? Dream again. Dream your dreams. Don't abandon what matters to you. Look up and don't give up yet. Have a "Fourth Quarter mentality" like the 2016 Chicago Cubs.

Many a fight, battle, game and so many accomplishments have been won in the fourth quarter when it seemed like it was already over. The time when teams or individuals are the most tired, the most worn down, and the most vulnerable is near the end of the game. It just takes extra courage, faith, and hope to stay the course.

Whatever weighs heavily on your heart and mind today, in the boardroom, the break room, the locker room, or the living room, I know it's been a long "three quarters." I realize this year's been up and down. The Fourth Quarter, whether it's truly the actual fourth quarter or not, you can always choose an MTXE fourth quarter mindset. It could be the moment when everything turns around for the better.

Get Quiet and Visualize
Your Most Desired Outcomes

In the midst of everything going south, do you find your "better" hard to see at the moment? I'd like to share a little exercise that takes just three minutes to do and it can make a world of difference. Olympians and professional athletes from the NFL, NBA and MLB all swear by its power to turn things around fast. It's called "visualization" and I mentioned it briefly way back in Chapter 1.

Go to a place where you can get quiet for three minutes or at least ignore the noise around you. Close your eyes and imagine things going right. Imagine the meeting going well with smiles all around. Imagine your presentation going well and the burst of applause at the end. Imagine your customers happily buying your product or service and thanking you for your help solving a thorny problem. See it in your mind like an imaginary movie trailer. Envision everything going perfectly. If you want to say a little prayer thanking God, that's even better. Then open your eyes, take a deep breath and get after it.

Scientists have proven visualization works. In fact, a study was done where three separate groups of college basketball players of equal skill levels were given an assignment. The first group put in extra free throw practice every day for thirty minutes in addition to regular practice. The second group visualized themselves shooting perfect free throws for five minutes a day in addition to regular practice. The third control group did nothing different.

After a one-month test the results were stunning. The group that visualized themselves shooting a perfect free throw improved every bit as much as the group which put in extra practice time. It can work like that in your professional life and your personal life, too.

Life Happens in Seasons

With HBO GO, Netflix, and Amazon, it's easy to binge-watch season after season of your favorite show. When you watch several seasons of a favorite show, in succession you pick up on subtle changes in the characters you love.

We all watched the Huxtable family grow up before our very eyes back in the day. We found ourselves feeling for Anthony Junior and Meadow Soprano, along with Tony and Carmella's many marital ups and downs. We pulled for Vinny Chase and the boys in Entourage, and we couldn't wait to see what Ari would do next.

We notice as characters grow and develop into their full potential. Even cute, little Rudy Huxtable grew up on the Cosby Show, and Christopher became a made man in The Sopranos. In the last season of Entourage, Turtle surprised us all and became a millionaire.

Though we find ourselves almost connected to these characters on the big screen, they're not real. It's just a TV show, but we still relate to them. Why? Because we know we must face the same kind of issues in our own lives. If you watched your life back through the seasons, I'm sure you'd notice subtle changes, developments, and growth, personally and professionally.

Maybe it's obvious, but I believe it's worth mentioning. In your life, you'll have great days and bad days. You'll have fun times and incredibly annoying situations to endure. You'll enjoy success one minute and struggle to find your way the next. You'll have good seasons and bad ones. When you're in an emotional valley it's easy to get a bad case of "woe is me." Catch yourself in those moments, and remember, it's just a season, This too shall pass. Life happens in seasons.

Keep looking up, being you, and do the right thing. Often you can look back and realize that's what got you where you are today.

Until the good Lord calls us home, and wraps this whole thing up, there's still time on the clock. There are days left on the calendar for this week, this month, and this year. Finish strong by encouraging someone, helping someone, lifting the

Keep looking up, being you, and do the right thing.

spirits of coworkers, family members, loved ones, students, friends, guests, clients, and customers. It truly does make a difference.

Fight Through it and Finish Strong

We've all been there and can picture it clearly. You're frustrated. It's Friday morning, and you're 100 percent over it. The weekend is on the other side of that last email, meeting, or phone call. You could relax and take it easy after lunch, right? Just mail it in from about 2:00 pm on and coast through the afternoon, going through the motions as you count the minutes until happy hour. Or, you could be awesome. It's up to you.

You could attack your "to do list" this morning right off the bat, first crack out of the box. Spend the first fifteen minutes of your day thinking about the most important things on your list. You're passin' where you need to pass and shootin' where you need to shoot.

"Eat that frog," as New York Times bestselling author, Brian Tracey says in his book of the same name. He says, "If the worst thing you have to do all day is to eat a live frog, then do it first; that way nothing else for the rest of the day could possibly be that bad."

Dale Carnegie said if you'll focus on doing the three most important things in your day first, you'll rise above others and enjoy success.

Consider your competition, whether they're Sales Managers of a rival company; Agents vying for the same clients; other entrepreneurs working on developing their billion-dollar idea; or the other applicant who's going for the same job as you. They'll probably mail it in after lunch. You could get ahead of the pack and finish strong, rather than slacking off just because it's Friday afternoon.

Think about your teammates, your peers, your staff, your spouse or even your boss. Could anyone use an extra hand completing a project? Brainstorming an idea? Drafting a proposal? If you've busted it this week so far and have a little extra capacity left over, offer your services to someone else.

That question you answered for someone on Tuesday? Call them back and ask how it turned out, whatever it may be. The client you said you'd get back to with an answer or proposal by the first of the week? Hit them with a surprise call on Friday afternoon with the good news. How about the staff member who came to you yesterday with a random question you couldn't answer? Get the answer and follow up with them before they take off for the weekend. You'll make them feel like a million bucks because you cared. You also position yourself as a person who has a reputation of following through on your promises. Taking extra steps like this for people also builds great relationships in both your career and personal life.

"Pain is Temporary, Pride is Forever!"

Or is it the other way around?

Athletes grow up seeing this slogan plastered on the walls inside locker rooms, gymnasiums, on the backs of tee shirts, or even across the backside of gym shorts. It means to fight through it. Fight through the temporary pain; the soreness, fatigue, and adversity because you'll be proud you did, knowing you fought the good fight.

Great slogan. It's probably true. The opposite is also probably true.

Let me explain.

When you're fatigued, tired, fed up, worn down, and super annoyed at your coworkers, significant others, bosses, clients, customers, or family members that irritation often stems from an underlying trigger. It's pride. When pride and ego bubble up to the surface, you run the risk of saying or doing things you don't truly mean and run a greater risk of hurting others, ultimately hurting yourself. All your work, effort, and potential unfortunately become null and void as pride and ego overshadow all the good you've done or intend to do. Why? Because you made other people feel awful about themselves, hurting their feelings in the process.

A temporary flare up of pride can cause pain forever. It comes in the way of lost relationships and sometimes even lost jobs. You lose the opportunities you might've otherwise had for career growth, personal growth and spiritual growth. When I screw up it's due to pride. I can think of three individuals right now I've hurt with momentary pride flare-ups. Those moments of pride have caused permanent pain in the way of lost relationships and opportunities. Poof. Gone. You can probably think of a few as

A temporary flare up of pride can cause pain forever.

well. If not, you're way ahead of the game.

Adversity happens around every corner. Remember, *how* you deal with those circumstances makes all the difference in the world. Fight through it and finish strong. You'll be glad you did, as meaningful relationships, incredible opportunities, and potential beyond your wildest dreams are also waiting for you right around the corner.

PART FOUR

KEEP YOUR RELATIONSHIPS IN PERSPECTIVE

CHAPTER 18

The East Carter High School MTXE Raider Basketball Camp was and still is the highlight of summer for many youngsters who grew up in my hometown. One morning when I was twelve, during the MTXE Basketball Camp, Coach Baker huddled all the campers upstairs along the running track that circles the gymnasium on the upper deck. He talked to us for about ten minutes before starting our practice drills downstairs. He shared his perspective about how we should prioritize the game of basketball relative to other vital, important relationships in our lives.

Keep the Main Thing the Main Thing

Coach told everyone it's okay for basketball to be important, but it's not the most important thing. He taught us how important relationships would be to all of us for the rest of our lives. He continued by recommending an order of importance for those ever-so-important relationships. Then he put into perspective where basketball should fall in the grand scheme of things:

- First and foremost, commit to and trust in a relationship with God.
- Second, make sure to focus on your relationships with family and friends.
- A distant third, in order of importance, was basketball and the relationships that come with it: teammates, coaches, fans, and even our competitors.

Remember how life and death sports used to feel when you were growing up? I mean, really. By the time Remember the Titans and Varsity Blues came out we all saw a little bit of ourselves in the characters in those movies. For me, it was basketball. For you, maybe it was cheerleading football, soccer, hockey, or lacrosse. So many of us were consumed by our sports.

We would eat, sleep, and breathe the game we loved, remember? We were always practicing or playing. When we weren't practicing or playing, we were thinking about practicing or playing the game. You'd sit and stew about a bad call, a choice word or an argument with a teammate, referee, coach, or competitor. You'd be in bed at night losing sleep, keyed up with visions of the play that almost was, or the pass that got away bouncing around in your head.

Then, once all those worries and anxieties died down, you'd get excited at the slightest thought of lacing 'em up again tomorrow. Remember looking forward to the next day, for the next practice, game? Or, pick-up games with friends in the offseason? That was the fun part.

That's my point. This whole thing about playing sports in the first place, started because it was supposed to be fun. Remember getting yourself all worked up talking about, thinking about, and obsessing about this facet or that one about your sport? Often, you'd find yourself not having any fun.

The hype and chaotic nature of any competition or fanfare usually brings along with it a good bit of worry, anxiety, and tension. Sound familiar? Sound a little like corporate America? Sound like your job and the pressures to perform and produce results where you work? The same thing happens to us today; just like when you were younger, playing sports.

You sit up at night and lose sleep, thinking about the conversation that went sideways at work. Or, that tense phone conversation with the boss, which once again didn't go your way. Chances are you tend to spend your precious time away from the office, neck bent ninety degrees, looking down and punching little letters with your fingers and thumbs on your smart phone. Whether you're typing emails or texting, you still obsess to your coworkers or bosses about work, work, work.

Just like Coach Baker taught me back at the MTXE Basketball Camp, in Grayson, Kentucky, we should prioritize what's most important. Sports were "our thing" when we were younger. Now it's about your job and career. Back in the day you were passionate about making jump shots, catching or hitting line drives, scoring touchdowns, enthusiastically performing in your sport of choice. Today, you obsess about performing in your role at work, impressing the bosses in the hope they'll acknowledge you, accept you, and hopefully promote you into a higher paying job.

Meanwhile, it's easy to lose sight of what's most important through all the hype, chaos, hustle, and bustle of the day-to-day grind. Late nights and early mornings at work encroach upon your time with family and loved ones. Or worse, when you're spending time with family after work or on your day off, you're still texting, emailing, and thinking about work stuff all day and night. As you get lost in it all, you have zero fun, which was the point and the reason you sought out the job in the first place. Not cool. Not okay.

Most of us made a concerted effort to pursue a specific type of job with a specific company because we thought we'd enjoy it. That's the same reason you started playing sports when you were nine and ten years old and on into high school. You figured you'd enjoy it. Yet all too often you're robbed of the fun you thought you'd have, or the fun you could be having. That's when you realize it's time for a different mindset, a different approach.

Have Faith

This section of Ballgames to Boardrooms is all about having fun. One of the easiest ways to begin having fun regardless of your situation is to start with the priorities outlined above.

First, trust God. Once you trust Him, lean into a relationship with Him. He's already pursuing you, no matter how many knucklehead things you might do. God not only loves you, but He wants a relationship with you. He loves us despite the fact we sometimes mess up, he already knows we'll probably mess up at some point. Yet He loves you and me anyway despite all our mistakes.

If you're a believer, you know how cool it is. You've felt the unexplainable feeling of God touching you, blessing you, and making a remarkable positive difference in your life. If you're not a believer, that's okay. It's okay to not be okay. And, it's truly okay to not have a relationship with God, but you don't have to stay that way.

First, trust God. Once you trust Him, lean into a relationship with Him.

Imagine a relationship in which no matter where, when, or how messed up the situation, someone always listens, loves, cares, and will be there to help you. Imagine doing the worst thing possible, and that same someone still loves you as much as He did before you did the worst thing imaginable.

That's God. He's here. He's there. Wherever you go next week, next month or next year, yeah, He'll be there too, loving you all the same. That's cool. And. That. Is. Fun!

When you have a relationship with God, and you put all your trust in where and how far He will take you while on this Earth, you can breathe a little easier. Worries and anxiety give way to blessings, peacefulness, and an abundance of joy because you know you'll end up in Heaven one day, reconnecting with loved ones you've lost on Earth, and celebrating "the wonders of his love" as the song goes.

We Know How this Story Ends (and Begins)

When you have a relationship with God, you know your time here on Earth is just a quick, twenty-second time out in comparison to the eternity of sports, boats, beaches, singing, dancing, and never ending sugar cookies, banana nut bread, and pound cake made by your grandmothers awaiting your arrival in Heaven. And carbs probably don't even count in Heaven.

I like to use an analogy of watching a replay of a game on DVR having already peeked at the final score. Since moving to the west coast, I miss most Kentucky Wildcat basketball games in real time. So, I DVR most of them. Of course, I always peek at the score before getting home to watch. It's amazing how much more relaxed I am, watching the Cats games already knowing the result, which is usually a Wildcat win by a massive margin.

For believers and those who have a relationship with God, you already know the end result. You already know what happens at the end of the game here on Earth. God wins. Since God wins, everyone wins, all because you have a relationship with Him.

That perspective and faith makes it a little easier to relax and have fun inside and outside work, doesn't it? Even the most worrisome, intense, awkward day in corporate America pales in comparison to how awesome things will be in the long run, with our number one relationship always number one in our life. That's truly living and working for an audience of one as mentioned earlier.

Look at the Big Picture

Another way to keep things fun is by carving out room for your family and friends. This goes for Moms, Dads, siblings, grandparents, aunts, uncles, and cousins just as much as it goes for whomever you consider the people who mean the most to you in your life. So, whether it's your own blood relatives or those with whom you've grown to know and love like family, be sure to carve out ample time to spend with them. It helps keep what's important in perspective.

My Mom was a schoolteacher in Eastern Kentucky for twenty-seven years. She taught her students including kindergarten, first, and second graders to always look at "the big picture." That kept things in perspective for her students at ages five, six, and seven who had worry after worry back then. By always looking "at the big picture" they kept things in perspective. It's a good reminder for us as busy, responsible, stressed-out adults, trudging through our daily grind at work.

Whether it's writing and sending one more email, or cranking out one more hour at work, in the long run, when you consider the big picture, it won't mean much. While the hustle we talked about earlier is important, strike the right balance. It's less important than the meaningful conversation you'll have with your Mom, Dad, Aunt, Uncle, or significant other waiting for you at home on the couch. Staying worked up about the boss who doesn't get it or your coworkers who always get by doing so little won't add any more years to your life. However, making sure you spend quality time with your family and loved ones to balance out all those stressful hours at work, will certainly add more life to your years.

That leaves your relationships at work in a distant third place. That's not to say relationships at work aren't important, because they're absolutely critical. I'm just suggesting when you keep God first, family second, and work a distant third, you're able to approach your career "work" with a cleaner, more focused state of mind.

It's amazing how much more relaxed you can be at work when you know you have a loving Heavenly Father. He's pursuing you, championing you, and encouraging you in the background. How about knowing you have a vacation, a dinner, or even a meaningful conversation over a beverage with a loved one or family member waiting for you on the other side of a tough conversation at work? Keeping it all prioritized and in perspective helps keep the difficult meetings, phone calls and corporate corporateness of it all from ruining your mood. That alone will make your work more fun. Which makes it easier to go the extra mile.

With what's important in order, you'll be more adept in accepting the organizational realities where you work. This allows you to appreciate coworkers, bosses, and your job for what it is and release what it's not. Far better than nitpicking their faults and letting them ruin your days. On the contrary, with your relationships in perspective and priorities in order, you'll be more likely to have compassion for your bosses, coworkers, employees, clients and even your competitors. That'll keep things more positive and uplifting at work, which makes it way more fun.

Keep God first:

- Pray

- Find a church or place of worship you like.
- Get to know the people who will become your "spiritual family."
- Lean into and experience the magic of a beautiful relationship with a Heavenly Father who always has and never will stop loving you

That will be fun.

Keep your family a close second:

- Call your mother or a "motherly figure" in your life. She'll make you feel better, even if you have different perspectives. In fact, that's the value of the call.
- Then, if you need a "make up" or "reconciliation phone call", it will strengthen your relationship along the way.
- Manage yourself from spending too much time at the office or at work.
- Remember, the most important people aren't the ones at work, they're the ones at home.
- Plan vacations – mini vacations and big ones – with family and loved ones.
- There's no better way to ensure work-life balance and to strengthen your most important relationships than spending time away.

That will be fun.

Keep work relationships thriving, but a distant third:

- Take time to have an occasional lunch with coworkers
- Get to know coworkers, bosses, and employees personally despite what conventional wisdom says about "making friends at work." If you want to be bored and hate seven out of eight hours of work, every day until you retire, sure, by all means don't get to know people at work.

- But if you want to have fun, lighten up the mood and engage. It's fun!
- Ask how you can help.
- Help them anyway, no matter how they answer the question above.
- Listen more than you talk. It's amazing how the very act of listening alone will strengthen your relationships.
- Celebrate wins with your team
- Love people as God loves you, and tell them you do. Seriously, make it awkward. If you put forth the effort to get to know people, there will be some who you just can't help but love. That can turn a dumb job into truly meaningful work.
- Don't forget to tell them you love them. You'll be surprised when they say it right back.

And. That. Will. Be. Fun.

DRAW UP A NEW PLAY

CHAPTER 19

How often do you find yourself watching a game, and it's back and forth, nip and tuck, ho hum, blah blah blah? Same routine, by both teams, on both sides of the ball. Your team has the ball then their team has the ball, and back and forth it goes.

Boring.

Take for example, your typical football game, when it's first and ten, and a little scampering run play gets the offense three yards. Now, second and seven, a slant across the middle picks up another two yards as your number one receiver gets form tackled in space, stopped in his tracks. So, it's third and seemingly a short five yards to go for the first down, and a hand-off run play gets stuffed for no gain.

Fourth down.

Punting unit trots onto the field, and lines up for yet another punt, on yet another fourth down. The ball is snapped, and the punter winds up to kick it into next week, but...OH!

Wait!

IT'S A FAKE! A FAKE PUNT!

The punter fakes a kick, turns on a dime, and sprints to a first down and more.

First down!

The game goes from boring to exciting with just one play. It's amazing how one play can completely change the complexion of a game or even a season, for individuals and teams.

New Plays are Purposeful

In basketball, football, or any team sport, often coming out of a timeout, quarter break, or halftime, the coach draws up a new play.

It's usually designed with purpose, to achieve a specific outcome. The obvious desired outcome is to score points. While that's often the case, great coaches peel back the layers of the onion and draw up new plays for other reasons, which add value in other ways.

A new play can be the spark that:

- Ignites a slumping player
- Unleashes the talent or extraordinary potential in an emerging star
- Catches the opposition off guard
- Builds confidence among the team when executed flawlessly
- Proves to each player involved they matter and they belong

New plays keep everyone, on both teams, on their toes, keeping the game fresh, exciting, and most importantly, FUN.

The same is true at work, trudging to and from the office, day in and day out, week after week, and before we know it, we blink, and we've been in the same role for several years. Today feels the same as it did when we started. Not very fun.

However, just like in that football example of a beautifully timed fake punt to absolutely disrupt the game, we can draw up new plays, at any time, for ourselves and for those around us, which turn menial jobs into meaningful work with some fun along the way.

We can disrupt the status quo, completely changing the complexion of our otherwise boring situation. Our friends, family, coworkers, and even our bosses will thank us for keeping them on their toes, and for making work fun again.

Consider this from a couple different perspectives - one as a leader of teams, and another perspective as a member of a team.

Draw Up a New Play as a Leader

Shuffle the Deck

Shake up who is responsible for what, among your team. Sometimes changing the responsibilities among your team can be just the purposeful disruption some individuals need to become reengaged, giving them newfound purpose and commitment to your team's mission. Fresh, outside perspectives add value because often when people are focused for so long on the same things, they can't see the trees for the forest.

Shaking things up will make an otherwise boring gig fun again. They'll also appreciate you for not only taking an interest in their work lives but also taking action to make their jobs less boring vs. playing it safe, refusing to shake things up, and enabling the most boring job ever to keep its title.

Disrupt Ordinary Routines

Routines and faithfulness to daily game plans are necessary. However, going long periods of time with the same old same old is risky because complacency has a way of rearing its ugly head in the all too familiar sea of sameness that is corporate America.

Don't let your team get complacent.

Don't let your team get complacent.

Call an out of the ordinary meeting, in a completely new meeting location, perhaps even outdoors. Ask a member of the team to facilitate or present something to the group. Let everyone go early one day, or tell them to come in late, while encouraging them to have breakfast with their families or sneak in a morning workout before coming to the office. You (and they) may be surprised at the boost in energy, focus, and urgency resulting from the disruption.

Try Something New

Recommend a new process or product to your senior leaders. Build the case, get some cross-functional alignment and agreement on your side, and call an impromptu boardroom scene meeting, ala The Apprentice. Just like drawing up a new play catches the opposition off guard in sports, it will have the same impact in business. That idea you've had for so long but been so hesitant to suggest could be the edge or competitive advantage your organization needs to win more market share or become more profitable. Taking some risks, out on the skinny branch, playing to win, is more fun than sitting back, playing it safe, playing not to lose.

Draw Up a New Play as a Member of a Team

Take Another Road

On a routine Wednesday, before or after work, take a different route to or from work, on purpose. The change in scenery will open your mind as new, fresh views of areas you haven't seen in a while get you thinking about new, fresh ways to go about solving that problem back at the office. Or while at work, instead of walking the same way to lunch, your meetings, or even the restroom, take a different route.

Walking a different route forces you out of your comfort zone, and puts you in situations to meet, engage with, and build community with people you otherwise wouldn't see if you just walk your same route every single day.

We used to do this working in huge mega-resorts in Las Vegas. Hotel veterans taught us to change up our routes when walking to and from meetings, from one side of the property to the other. It was a money move. This way, we took in more of the property, got to know our product better, and engaged with more and more people over time. It worked! It kept things fresh and exciting.

Write a Handwritten Note

Write a handwritten note of gratitude or encouragement to someone in your office. This changes up the energy in the air right away. Nobody does it anymore, and what's worse is people deserving of those notes of gratitude or encouragement rarely feel appreciated or encouraged. When you do things no one bothers to do anymore, it gets noticed. It's amazing how good a handwritten note makes people feel. That goes for both the deliverer and the recipient.

I once received a handwritten note from the General Manager of a hotel thanking me for delivering an inspirational message to our Front Desk team, and I was on cloud nine for two weeks. It felt amazing to know that he noticed me and knew that I was pouring my heart and soul into the resort and its staff.

Years later, I delivered a handwritten note of gratitude to the CEO of The Cosmopolitan of Las Vegas when I worked there on the grand opening team. A week later I found myself sharing an elevator ride with him! With a firm handshake and a pat on the back, he said, "Thanks so much for your note. I had a bad morning this morning, and I got your card back out of my desk and read it again. It picked me right back up." I just smiled and tried to act like his comment and personal acknowledgment wasn't causing a lump in my throat and tears to well up behind my eyes. I was so touched that he was touched, and I'm certain that moment and those feelings would have never happened if not for me writing that note.

Volunteer to Lead a Project

Our leaders run ragged, week after week, trying to deliver for their leaders, all the way up the food chain. We find ourselves doing the same in our roles. Operative word, "same." Volunteering to lead a project or to take on anything new will not only break up the monotony of the grind for you, but it will also take your leaders by pleasant surprise to know they have an ally, advocate, and confidante in you. It's never ever a bad thing to achieve this dynamic with your boss.

You'll not only add tremendous value for your leaders, you'll also find a new bounce in your step. Suddenly you find yourself willingly rearranging your morning routine so you can get to the office earlier as opposed to reluctantly dragging yourself into the office just before you're supposed to arrive. You work out new "mental muscles," skills, and competencies you know are in your tool kit, but few people have ever seen in action. Most importantly, work becomes fun again in the process.

Have the courage to draw up new plays at work. Disrupt the day-to-day grind, and you'll find it less of a grind and way more fun.

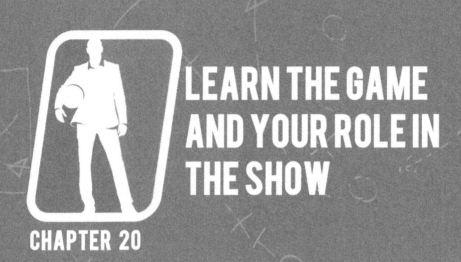

LEARN THE GAME AND YOUR ROLE IN THE SHOW

CHAPTER 20

Lebron James is an all-time NBA great. Whether you love him or hate him, we can all agree he's a phenomenon. His linebacker physique, cat-like quickness, six-foot eight-inch frame, and springs in his legs make him special, for sure. However, the extent to which he has and continues to study the game puts him in another echelon of greatness. He was a little smarter; a step quicker, and more effective than anyone else on the court during his high school years, and the same is true today, as he owns the court on any given night in the NBA.

Be a Student of the Game

Lebron and great professionals like him have figured out that while talent, skill, and hustle are important, becoming and remaining true students of their craft is usually the critical ingredient setting them apart from their peers, making them successful, and allowing them to maximize the enjoyment they get from the game, season after season.

Understanding and executing on the details of the game, be it basketball, football, soccer, hockey, or any other sport, is often the difference in winning and losing, being successful or merely average, or emerging as an influencer versus getting stuck on the sidelines.

For example, in the 2013 Eastern Conference Championship Series, Lebron and the Miami Heat were down one with 2.2 seconds remaining in overtime. Lebron tells the story about how in the split second just before the inbound play for their chance to win the game at the buzzer, he noticed Paul George of the Indiana Pacers leaning the slightest bit to his left leaving him in a less than ideal defensive stance. Lebron caught the inbound pass with his back to the basket, and quickly spun to his right with a man-child dribble for an instant highlight, not only exploiting his opponent's moment of weakness but also winning the game in dramatic fashion.

Lebron won that game, and then went on to lead the Heat to the 2013 NBA Championship. Lebron is one of the world's best because he has always been and continues to be a true student of the game. We should all be such students of our own "game", diving into and understanding the details of our industries, the dynamics of our operations, the drivers of our businesses, and most importantly how to execute on the levers that propel our teams to success.

Here are three compelling reasons to dive in, roll up your sleeves, and really "learn the game" and your role in the show, no matter where you work or where you are on the organizational chart. All these will result in your ability to have more fun doing what you do as opposed to feeling like you take spin after spin after spin running in circles like a hamster on a wheel. Remember:

- Learning is fun
- Eliminate unknowns
- Being good helps

Learning is Fun

You're probably questioning and maybe even making fun of my assertion that "learning is fun". My mom was my Kindergarten teacher, and I grew up with educators and public school administrators for aunts, grandmothers, and cousins. So maybe my opinion on learning is a bit biased. However, consider it in the context of where you currently work or maybe even where you want to work. Adding to your repertoire, sharpening your sword, acquiring new skills and competencies make you better today and more marketable for tomorrow.

Which is more fun? Getting asked to lead a project or getting asked to follow someone else's lead on a project? Which sounds better? Getting promoted in a year or getting stuck in your current circumstance at this same pay grade while others grow, making more money, flying to NYC or LA or Chicago for long weekends with friends or family?

Learn the game where you work, apply what you learn, and you'll find yourself adding tremendous value to your peers, your boss, and to your organization. When you add that kind of value, consistently, you become as indispensable as Lebron was to the Miami Heat and to the Cleveland Cavs. When you're indispensable, you max out your worth, and maxing out your worth maximizes how much you get paid.

When you couple learning your craft to a level of mastery along with going the extra mile, building positive relationships and all these tactics we learned from our coaches in sports, the difference can be remarkable. Money isn't the most important thing, but certainly we can all agree making more of it, getting paid what you're worth, is quite fun.

Eliminate Unknowns

All too frequently the thing keeping us from fully enjoying any experience is worry, or our own anxieties. We often worry about things we cannot control or that which is unknown. So, develop an undying thirst to learn as much as possible about your business, making you more and more knowledgeable with time. The more you learn, the more knowledge you have, and the more knowledge you have the more power and ability you gain.

If you're constantly learning, paying attention to relational data – cause and effect stuff like if X happens Y results; you'll rarely be caught off guard. Instead, worries are replaced with confidence because you know exactly what moves to make and when, regardless of the situation.

Think about the best leaders and coworkers with whom you've felt most comfortable working in past roles. Chances are the person or people you're thinking about right now were the best because they could effortlessly lean into any situation with confidence and ability, making decisions, taking appropriate action, and rarely getting stumped as to what to do.

They didn't just twinkle their nose one day and automagically become confident. No way. You can believe they put in the time, as true students of their trade or their craft, and learned the game. They not only made it a point to learn the game, but also how best to leverage their strengths as a complement to others' strengths, which put the team in the best position to achieve success.

The more we learn the more unknowns are transformed into fundamental understandings, and the more we understand the less time we spend worrying. Any time we spend less time worrying, we're left with more time to, yep, you guessed it, HAVE FUN.

Being Good Helps

Simply put, when you're good, it helps.

It just helps in so many areas of our lives – at work, at home, and in the community. When you've established credibility among the tribe – a team, an organization, or community – navigating becomes easier. When you have an idea, people will listen. When you give feedback, people will apply it. When you have a request, it's most likely granted. When you give praise, it is far more meaningful, when you've established credibility.

The quickest way to get the street cred is to simply be good at what you do. Nothing fancy. Whatever you're doing, whether you love it or hate it, just get good at it. Being good helps, and it's hard to get good at your craft without spending time learning it as a true student of the game, ala Lebron, Michael, or Magic.

What does "learning the game and your role in the show" look like? Here's a quick snapshot. True students of their craft do the following things without fail, every chance they get:

- Ask questions and when they ask, they listen intently.

- Observe others – high performers, low performers, and mediocre performers, taking note of what they do well, what they could do better, and what makes them great, terrible, or just average.
- They try new things, fail fast, course correct on their own, and try again, and again, and again until they're the Lebron of their craft.
- Seek feedback from people in various aspects of their lives – their own leaders, leaders of others, their peers, their friends, family, and even strangers.
- Apply the feedback, making changes where necessary in a constant pursuit of excellence.
- Flat out execute, every single day, with no excuses.
- Become self-aware with personality tests such as Myers Briggs, DISC, True Colors, or through old-fashioned conversations with others, learning how their personality traits reveal themselves in specific situations.
- Once aware of their personality traits, they're intentional about managing their emotions, tempering what comes out of their mouths, while remaining focused on what they can control.
- Finally, they know their core competencies, their strengths, and they leverage them as much as possible, leaving others to focus on areas in which they're not as strong.

Whatever your role and whatever your industry, craft, or trade, become a true student of it. Gain knowledge giving you the confidence to gain the credibility necessary to navigate easily through your day-to-day. You'll worry less, smile more, and with 100% certainty HAVE MORE FUN along the way.

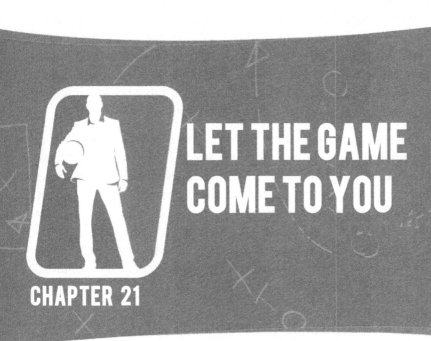

LET THE GAME COME TO YOU

CHAPTER 21

It was senior night, a chilly February Kentucky evening, at East Carter High School for my last home basketball game as an East Carter Raider. We weren't very good, but God bless our hometown fans, they all came out to support us at every home game. It seemed like the gym was buzzing more than usual, since it was senior night. One other senior and I would be recognized and honored before the game.

Traditionally, on senior night, the seniors walk out to center court, stopping by their families for an embrace along the way, before standing out at half court facing the crowd as the public-address announcer reads a short bio of statistics and accomplishments on and off the court. It's very cool, and at the ripe old age of seventeen, it was a huge deal to me. Few things in my childhood and adolescent years meant as much to me as basketball. It went, God, my family, school, and maybe tied for third was hoops.

With all the hype, giving my Mom a rose on the walk out, hugging my Dad, grandparents, and some little fellas who looked up to me at the time, there I went, strutting out to the middle of the court. The crowd buzzed, and when they announced my name, as I started my walk, it felt like the place erupted with cheers. Meanwhile, it probably didn't. But to me, at seventeen, that night might as well have been Game 7 of the NBA Finals, and I was basically Michael Jordan.

I was so amped, fired up to put on a good show for the fans, and end my regular season high school basketball career on a high note. Though we weren't a great team, I had my fair share of decent games throughout my career, averaging around fifteen points and eight assists per game with the occasional rebound and steal to round out the stat sheet (but who's counting...). I saw so many familiar faces in the bleachers, standing and cheering during the senior night festivities as we got set for the jump ball just before the game tipped off. I couldn't wait to get after it, and leave my indelible legacy as an East Carter Raider.

With visions of getting hot, probably dropping 20 or 25 points and my usual eight to ten assists, dazzling the crowd and firing up my teammates with electrifying behind-the-back, no-look passes, the ball was tipped. Off we went. My final home basketball game was underway.

And...it was bad. I played terribly.

I'm talking, really awful.

I couldn't buy a bucket. I had a million turnovers, and we lost.

Awesome.

Nearing the end of the third quarter, Coach Baker called me over, and said, "Relax. You're pressing too much, trying to force it."

Ya think!?!?!

Oh man, it was bad. I felt so bad and embarrassed. Meanwhile, the fans and our hometown faithful probably weren't really let down at all. I had just put all this pressure on myself for pretty much no reason other than my own ego!

Here's the Thing About Pressure

The same thing tends to happen as adults, in corporate settings at work. Things get so hyped up with our executives and senior leaders sending out their notes from high on executive mountaintops. Guests, customers, and clients can be quite demanding with their lofty expectations. Our teams need and expect the world from us, and we're go-getters, so we expect the world from ourselves.

We want to crush it. We have visions of nailing the project, exceeding expectations, winning over the bosses, delivering for our teams, and ascending the ladder every six months.

People feel the pressure. While some team members lean into it and crush life every day because they're more talented, more prepared, and have great work ethic, other, less talented or less committed people show their insecurities daily. They just might believe they're second-class players, unfortunately. Defense mechanisms, passive aggressive comments, dissension, and bitterness take over. Soon, we find ourselves in another unpleasant situation at work, yet again, having zero fun. Ever.

Once in high school, I told my Dad how much pressure I felt to deliver for my team, make good grades in school, and become successful. He told me, "That's just pressure you put on yourself." As usual, he was right. He's still right.

The same principle applies today at work and in life.

We put so much pressure on ourselves, to perform and deliver and win. Maybe it's our society but perhaps it's our own egos. Actually, not just "maybe." Usually our pride and ego creep up into our otherwise humble, fun-loving, childlike faith. Here comes pride and ego again, preventing us from enjoying the blessings in our lives.

With the pressure comes the need to control. It's human nature. We're all guilty of trying to control everything and everyone from time to time; especially when the stakes are high. Those two culprits, pride and ego, grab us, convincing us that

Comparing ourselves with others is the sure way to feeling disappointed, unhappy and critical of ourselves.

we know best, our way is better, and nobody else can do it as well as we can. We hold on so tightly, squeezing the life out of the controls, and in doing so we squeeze all the fun out of our lives! Comparing ourselves with others is the sure way to feeling disappointed, unhappy and critical of ourselves.

Good news! There's a better way.

Coach Baker and I'm sure many other coaches across all sports tell their players to *relax and let the game come to you.* Forcing the issue, trying to impose your will on the game, situation, relationship, meeting, or project is a recipe for frustration and burn out.

Here are three ways to let go of the controls and *let the game come to you,* as opposed to trying to control every single little thing. Enjoy better days with less frustration and more fun when you:

- Relax and play.
- Know your strengths. Leverage them and stay within them.
- Trust the process.

Relax and Play

Coach John Calipari is not shy with his sideline antics, during the University of Kentucky Wildcat basketball games. I loved his book, "Players First – Coaching from the Inside Out." He talked about this in his book, and he certainly walks the talk as one of his most common urges (or screams) from the sidelines during Cats games is, "Play!"

He wants his players to *play.* With all the hype, hoopla, and pressure, he never wants his players to lose sight of why they picked up the game in the first place, FUN. After all, they're talented, they work hard, and his players are usually very good. What a shame it would be for all that talent and hard work to go to waste. If it's not put to good use and put into practice, then what's the point?

All too often players get in their own way, putting too much pressure on themselves, preventing them from performing up to their potential, which keeps them from having fun.

Sad.

By the same token, the same thing happens to us in the workplace. Obviously, we were better than other candidates for our job. If we weren't they would've chosen someone else. So, we're capable. Clearly the bosses think we can do it because they keep sending the requests, questions, directives, and deliverables to us. They trust us.

Remember how good you are. You're a first-class player.

Don't forget how hard you've worked to get here. That same effort, talent, skill, and work ethic will allow you to deliver today, tomorrow, and down the road in your next gig. Relax. Relax and "play." Take the pressure off yourself, and instead tell the person in the mirror that he or she is capable and trusted. Take a deep breath, relax, and lean into your own capabilities. Then, just enjoy crushing it, just like you always have. You'll have way more fun.

Know Your Strengths.
Leverage Them and Stay Within Them

Remember the whole thing about keeping your passers passin' and your shooters shootin'? Now's a great time to bring it back up. Too often when pressure mounts, we press and press ourselves to do it all. Well, that's too much. You can't do it all. You can try, and you may be able to do it all for short stints and sprints, but as awesome as you are, you can't sustain doing it all for the long term. Trust me. I've tried. Doesn't work. You crush it for a week, month, or even a quarter, but eventually you flame out, burn out, and then come close to freaking out!

So don't do it. Just stay within your wheelhouse. Stay around the ball, but with everything you do, simply be aware of what you do best, and always offer that up to your boss, teammates, Guests, customers, and clients.

Know your strengths. For example, if you know you're great at math, stick to being the "numbers person". If you can write, volunteer to draft communications, take notes, write up proposals, or game plans for yourself, your teammates, or even your boss. If you nail it on presentations and love public speaking, hand raise for opportunities to train, coach, or even deliver presentations to audiences where you work.

Staying within yourself, leveraging your strengths, not only keeps you efficient and productive, it also shows you're self-aware.

Emotional intelligence is such a corporate America buzz phrase, but I must admit, it's one of the biggest keys to success for individuals and teams. Emotional intelligence is simply being aware of yourself – your emotions, strengths, weaknesses, and tendencies, for better or worse – and intentional about how you manage yourself and your emotions from one situation to the next. Everybody talks about emotional intelligence but few completely understand it and act on its ever-important principles.

Peers and leaders will notice you stepping up, volunteering where you're strong. That will be different from the insecure, average person who thinks they have to be a "know it all" about everything, aiming to grandstand in meetings and in every conversation in between so they're accepted by the boss or their peers. Let them be irritating. You be comforting.

Understanding your strengths, and being intentional about how and when to apply them takes the pressure off, little by little, day after day. A little pressure off here, and less stress there, accepting where you can and cannot add ample value frees up your mental capacity.

Then you optimize your skills, talents, and time to absolutely kill it on things you know are your cup of tea. Giving yourself permission to let others lead in other areas also takes the pressure off, allowing you to enjoy the ride, and you guessed it, have more fun along the way.

Trust the Process

One of my favorite shows of all time is The Profit, on CNBC. Marcus Lemonis is the star of the show. He's the CEO of Camping World and invests his own money to help small businesses. Episodes of The Profit document his investment projects. He does it to save jobs and to make money. He simplifies business principles for struggling entrepreneurs, teaching them to focus on three main things, people, process and product.

Usually the processes are broken, the people are a mess, and the product lines are in complete disarray. Enter Marcus and his teams to save the day. He works miracles with the people - teaching, coaching, encouraging, and developing individuals and teams. Together they scrap the current, failing processes, and create new ones. They simplify product offerings, and next thing you know, the businesses become profitable and everyone is happy; at least most of the time. Marcus coaches people to, "Trust the process."

In your day-to-day, you may or may not have a daily game plan or your own processes. If you don't, create them. Organize your day. Well-crafted daily game plans and your own processes will keep you focused in areas you find most valuable such as staying physically fit, inspired, prepared, informed, knowledgeable, approachable, and capable.

Think about your eight to ten hours at work each day, and consider the hour or two before and after work. How do you spend your time? If you're not sure, it's probably because you don't have set processes to keep you disciplined with your time management.

We always intend to do the right thing or productive things, but reality sets in and there we go. We get frustrated, stressed, and reach for a cocktail, Netflix, or our social media feeds, all of which giving us shots of dopamine, taking us off task. Then we get behind on our work, we aren't prepared, we're less informed, and then we get frustrated because we're so behind where we could or should be. I'm exhausted thinking about it. All this leads, once again, to no fun at work, at home, or anywhere in between.

Maybe you have a daily game plan. Perhaps you do have well-crafted processes for yourself, your team, and even your household. You know and they know exactly who does what by when, or at least who's supposed to. Maybe you work for a well-established, profitable business, organization, or corporation. Or, perhaps you work for a successful small business in your town, and the processes are tight. Excellent. You're ahead of the game.

Yet, you still find yourself frustrated, second-guessing peers, leaders, and yourself. The pressure mounts with those lofty expectations, and you try to control every little thing again (and so do I).

Chill. Trust the process.

Once you, your leaders, your peers, or long-standing, sustainable and profitable business where you work have processes set, trust them. They worked before, and they'll work again. If they don't, no problem, you can scrap them and start over. The important thing will be that at least you'll have processes and daily game plans as opposed to flying blindly without them.

Trust the process. You'll stress less and enjoy more, having more fun along the way.

ENJOY THE RIDE

CHAPTER 22

This entire book is a metaphor, threading and connecting sports to real life, focusing on corporate settings as a big part of life. Here's another metaphor, but this time I'll use roller coasters – as an example of your Work Life and your "Life life."

Here's the illustration: compare your life to a roller coaster. Does this sound familiar?

Up…Down…Slow Down…Speed Up…
Twists…Turns…Fun Times (during the fast, fun downhill
part)…but not without nervous anticipation (during the
climb)… Bumpy, shaky, rough patches while spinning,
turning through the loops…followed by smooth transitions
back to a satisfying, fun, and exciting cruise as we glide
back to where we started…

Every single time, after any ride, the first thing you probably think and say is, "Wanna go again?"

We quickly forget about our nervous anticipation. The memory of the bumpy, shaky rough patches is short-lived. The helpless, scary feeling of spinning out of control was frightening, but you survived. It was all worth it to experience those precious moments of awesome. We remember and hang on to the fun moments, racing down the hill, "taking flight," laughing, smiling, and genuinely enjoying the ride.

You Get One Life on Earth so Enjoy It

Our lives, both at home and at work, are a similar ride, complete with the same Ups, Downs, Twists, Turns, Bumpy rough patches, and fun moments, when our careers, friendships, relationships, and experiences truly "take flight."

When the bumpy rough patches, nervous moments, and unexpected twists and turns roll into your life; remember they'll be short-lived. Think, "This too shall pass."

Sure, life gets in the way and many situations are tough to navigate. Bad days are an unfortunate reality. They happen. Wherever you are in life and through whatever "rough patches" you face in between the fun times, remember this mental OneMoreStep:

You can ride a roller coaster again and again by simply getting back in line. However in life, the job, the friendships, the relationships, and the experiences you have today may not last forever.

So, no matter how bumpy it gets, enjoy the ride. If you don't take that mental OneMoreStep to appreciate and enjoy each season of life, you'll probably look back one day and wish you did. You may have that familiar desire to "go again..." but it might be too late.

Here are a few ways to consciously enjoy the ride:

- Try to celebrate the victories, big and small
  - o Reward yourself

o   Recognize and praise others
- Embrace the beauty of "now"

Celebrate the Victories, Big and Small

In sixth grade, our basketball coach, Donald Damron, was awesome. We ran the table that year. We only played seven or eight games, but we won them all. Sometimes we played well, and sometimes we just played okay. Often, he encouraged and praised us for playing hard, executing our game plan, and hustling. Like any good coach, he'd also rip us if we weren't hustling or executing. It was so cool, after games even when we didn't play all that great but got the win anyway, Coach Damron always paused before his postgame speech, and said, "Let's take a minute to celebrate the victory."

We'd all give a collective, "Yaaaaaahhhhhhhh!!!"

Reward Yourself

You work hard. Even if you're not going all out 100 percent of the time, at times you know you crush it. You deserve a nice reward. We all have moments when hard work pays off. You make the grade, get a great year-end review, make a sale, complete a project, nail it on a task, or sometimes you just flat-out execute, firing on all cylinders from snap to whistle on a given day, week, month, or even a quarter.

Reward yourself.

When you've been disciplined, executed the game plan according to what you or your boss laid out, and accomplished an individual or team goal, take a well-deserved break. I know it sounds simple and elementary, but few people do it. Making an effort to celebrate the victories at work and in your personal life is important. The reality is corporate America and even society, to a certain extent, won't stop the clock for you to make sure you're rewarded when you deserve it. Sometimes, maybe. But not all the time. Here are a few ways to reward yourself:

- Give yourself permission to take a well-deserved break.
- Travel – take a weekend trip or a staycation to enjoy life for a minute.

- Splurge – reward yourself with a little present, to you from you; something you've had your eye on for a while but couldn't quite justify the purchase.
- Eat, Drink, and be Merry. It's amazing how enjoyable a great meal with a well-crafted cocktail, craft beer, or nice glass of wine can be. Take time to enjoy quality food and beverages.
- Just be. We stay in a constant worn out state, so when you've just crushed it on something, give yourself permission to. Just. Be. For a minute or two. Relax. You've earned the right to do so.

Recognize, Congratulate, and Praise Others

- Handwritten Notes – we've already established this lost art to *draw up a new play*. It's a great way to recognize others – your peers, your team, your boss, or even your friends and family. One holiday season I received a text message from one of my best friends. It was a picture of a holiday card I had sent him from ten years prior, which he found in an old shoebox as he was cleaning out his closet. He was touched, reading it again. I was touched at what I wrote ten years prior. But I became frustrated with myself because while those heartfelt sentiments I shared in my note were important and meaningful to us both, I realized it had been a while since I'd written a note like that to a friend, a family member, or my team. Take time to do this more. It's a lost art, and a low-cost way to make a huge positive impact on someone else.
- Emails. Use them for both public and private notes of recognition, congratulations, and praise. Everyone's on their phones most of the time, and everyone in corporate or business settings uses email as their number one mode of communication. My mom always says, "Meet people where they are." It sounds simple, but if and when we recognize people via email, it's immediate, efficient, and if presented appropriately, it's impactful.
- Promote people. Give people the promotion they deserve. It sounds simple, but too often folks on our team or high-

performers on another team deserve a promotion, yet we wait for the right time to do so. We wait until the next fiscal year, when we have the budget, approved headcount, or until we find out our high-performer is interviewing with other firms. Be bold. If they deserve it, advocate for them with your own leaders and let them know you're doing so. Nothing makes a young, up and comer feel more valued and appreciated than knowing their boss is going to bat for them with the big bosses. Once my direct leader at Disney Destinations told me after my first year with him in Sales he was going to talk to his boss about bumping me up to "Sr. Sales Manager." I might as well have been told I'd been granted a C-suite gig with stock options, company car, clothing allowance, and an executive compensation package. I felt appreciated and valued, which led to staying on board, focused, and motivated to drive business for those same leaders who promoted me a few months later.

- Give them more responsibility. Sometimes promotions are deserved, but I get it. Budgets are tight, executives are held to lofty EBITDA goals, and you're not going to win a debate to promote your ringers. Fine. Give them more responsibility, something for them to own. They'll feel just as awesome knowing you trust them. They'll know they've officially *earned the ball*. Their sense of purpose and passion will spike, and their performance will continue driving your business forward.

- Give them more autonomy. When leaders let go, and give their people room to run with it, people know with 100 percent certainty, they're trusted and valued. This is hard because a leader must be confident and comfortable enough to let go. I like what Eric Chester says in his book, "On Fire at Work," "Trust people before you know you can." It's true. Sometimes up and comers won't step up and lean into their talent until they know it's on their shoulders to deliver. So, let them perform without hovering over them. You'll be surprised with their level of engagement and their performance when they nail it.

Embrace the Beauty of Now

No matter what you have going on in your life right now, these truths apply:

- You'll never be younger than you are right now.
- If that "imminent thing" you're dreading is looming, it's still just that, looming. If it hasn't happened yet - why worry?
- The annoying disappointments of yesterday are gone, in the past. You don't have to keep dealing with them now.
- Most of what you learned in school or in life can finally be put to use, right now.
- Even if you haven't quite accomplished your goals, you can hustle and work toward making your dreams a reality, now.
- If you're in a rut, or a rough patch; it's only a season. It won't be this way forever.
- If life is good, and you're enjoying it, you'll soon miss the way things are, right now.

The moments that make us happy are never more wonderful than when they're happening. Sure, you have the memories, and pictures of what happened, but our most cherished moments capture our hearts and minds, right now as they're happening.

So instead of worrying about what might happen, or the unfortunate things that have happened, focus on what's happening now. Too often we don't enjoy what's happening now, and we find ourselves asking, "What happened?" Then, all we can think about is how good we had it "back in the day."

I like what our friend Andy Bernard said in one of his last monologues on NBC's The Office – Series Finale:

"I wish there was a way to know you're in the 'good ole days' before you've actually left them."

~ Andy Bernard

You can dream about how it should be, how it's supposed to be, or how you'd like it to be. OR, accept and embrace how things are, right now, today; because what's happening in this moment is real. It's not a dream.

That's what makes NOW beautiful. It may be a mess, but at least it's not a fantasy. Embrace it. Accept it. Enjoy it. Love it. Love the NOW, because later you may look back and wish you embraced more, accepted more, enjoyed more, and loved more.

Coach Baker and I were texting about this book project. I told him about the five parts. He commented on the "Have Fun" piece and efficiently summed up the principle. Simply put, he said, "If you don't enjoy, you and everyone around you will be miserable."

We've all been there, and we can all agree it's no fun.

Remember to enjoy the ride!

PART FIVE

MAKE THE EXTRA PASS (UNLEASH COMPASSION)

MAKE THE EXTRA PASS

CHAPTER 23

It was Game 6 in the 1997 NBA Championship Series. The Chicago Bulls were up three games to two on the Utah Jazz. The Bulls had won the championship in 1991, 1992, and 1993, of course. The Houston Rockets won it in 1994 and 1995, in large part, because Michael Jordan retired for the first time during those two years. The Bulls won it all in 1996, Michael's first full year back from retirement. Now, here they were on the world's biggest basketball stage in early June with a chance to win it all for the fifth time in seven seasons.

Game 6 was back and forth the whole way, a very close game in which every shot was a big shot, every pass a critical one, and every call a big call. If the Bulls won, the 1997 NBA Finals Championship would belong to them once again. If the Jazz won the game, the series would extend to a seventh and final Game.

The game was tied at 86, and the Bulls had the ball. Coming out of a timeout, Michael Jordan told the team and Head Coach, Phil Jackson, "Gimmie the ball. I'll win it."

Everyone in the arena, at bars, restaurants, and everyone in living rooms across the globe knew the ball was going to Michal Jordan for the inevitable instant classic for which sports fans had grown to love and expect in the 1990's. "Jordan with a game-winner" had become quite commonplace.

Jordan was "the man." He lived for it. And we lived for it.

Here was the scene: Twenty seconds to go in the game, with every fan on the edge of their seat or completely out of their seat. The Bulls run a play. It was a little motion offense; Point Guard, Steve Kerr walks the ball up the floor, Scottie Pippen pops out to the left wing as Kerr zips him the ball. Michael, always moving without the ball, dashes, cuts, and breaks open, finally getting the ball in his hands. Here we go. This is what the Bulls wanted, and it's what Michael lived for, being "the man." It's what the world was waiting for, its next poster-able image of the world's greatest basketball player of all time taking the last second shot to win the championship in dramatic fashion yet again.

You Don't Have To Do It All

Michael makes his move, takes a couple dribbles around his defender, and we're just waiting for His Airness to launch, take flight, and do something magical. He had that look in his eyes, and in a split second, we got our instant classic.

But it wasn't Michael Jordan who took the shot.

Multiple Utah Jazz players collapsed on Michael's first few dribble moves toward the basket. Though he probably could have gone up with a dipsy do, up-and-under, double clutch shot, which only MJ could pull off, he didn't.

He made the extra pass.

Coming out of the huddle, teammate, Steve Kerr, had told Michael, "If they leave me and double team you, I'll be ready." Sure enough, that's exactly what happened.

With five seconds on the clock, and with his patented leap into the air, Michael saw Steve Kerr out of the corner of his eye at the top of the key. Rather than taking the shot, he kicked it to Kerr who caught it in rhythm from fifteen feet, and knocked down maybe the most beautiful jump shot in NBA history.

It was money. Literally "nothing but net."

Boom.

The Bulls won their fifth championship, once again, in storybook fashion. Steve Kerr would go down in history as the one who made the game-winner. Not Michael Jordan.

In the middle of the pressure to perform for our bosses, Guests, customers, and clients, or even for your family and friends, it's easy to think it all rests on your shoulders. Once again, here comes the need to control, and we instinctively go into protective mode. We not only try to "protect and defend" our stances on issues or the moves we make, but we also tend to become consumed with, well, ourselves. We think we must be "the Michael Jordan" of the moment, "the man" or "the woman", to make everything happen on our own.

We think if it's going to get done, we must be the ones to make every single move. This is also a trap. Don't give into it. Guard against thinking it's all on you, all the time. Whether you work on a team or as an individual contributor, remember you never look bad making somebody else look good. If Michael Jordan, in all his "Airness" and awesomeness, can make the extra pass, so can you and I.

Especially for leaders or those who aspire to become leaders, it's less about what you can do, and all about how well you can inspire and motivate others to achieve a goal, an objective, or simply reach their full potential. The ability to inspire is often a function of how well you connect. Remember in Chapter 15, you maximize your value adds to the team when you open up and have more meaningful conversations. Connection rarely happens unless or until you foster a relationship. Finally, relationships don't just happen overnight. They take work. A fast pass to gain productive relationships is, always has been, and always will be the ability to compromise.

Consider how dictionary.com defines the word *compromise*.

Noun:

1. A settlement of differences by mutual concessions; an agreement reached by adjustment of conflicting or opposing claims, principles, etc., by reciprocal modification of demands.
2. The result of such a settlement.
3. Something intermediate between different things

Compromise is such an important concept, but it's so much more. It's almost a prerequisite for any relationship to blossom, thrive, and become meaningful. Compromise is also an action. Without compromise, collections of talented or even not-so-talented individuals very seldom completely transform into fully functioning groups or high-performing teams. In other words, compromise allows for any partnership, group, team, or even nations to realize their full potential.

America's First Boy Band Found a Way to Compromise

For example, the very reason Americans today can proudly stand and sing our national anthem, "...the land of the free, and the home of the brave..." is because our founding fathers, who by all accounts were constantly at odds, disagreeing on issues, ultimately found a way to compromise. The most famous and perhaps most significant compromise of all time is The Constitution of the United States.

Consider America's first boy band. Thomas Jefferson, George Washington, James Madison and Alexander Hamilton. History teaches us, the boys certainly didn't agree with each other 100 percent of the time. In fact, they didn't even like each other much. This probably sounds all too familiar to your situation at work or in your company, in the political mess that is corporate America. But as Lin Manuel Miranda's *Hamilton – An American Musical* portrays, "...Two Virginians and an immigrant (Thomas Jefferson, James Madison, and Alexander Hamilton), walk into a room, diametrically opposed, foes..." They emerge from the *"room where it happened"* with a compromise in which both sides gave up something so our young nation would and could eventually have things like, um, a beautiful capital called Washington D.C., and a financial system which has allowed the United States to not only survive but thrive for over 240 years. It never would have happened without compromise.

Think of it as "Compro-My's." What we often forget about relationships, at work or otherwise, is a thriving relationship takes real work to achieve.

Compro-My's and Work

Sound familiar?

- You're wasting *my* time.
- This is a waste of *my* money.
- I hope this doesn't ruin *my* chances.
- How is this possibly good for *my* career?
- I shouldn't have to share any of *my* stuff.

Without compromise, relationships at the office and in our personal lives are impossible, and won't work. This means giving up something of our own; our time, our money, our stuff, or our own interests for something or someone beyond ourselves. It sounds magical enough, but we'd all agree it's often difficult to do.

The reality is, it takes real work.

> *Without compromise, relationships at the office and in our personal lives are impossible, and won't work.*

We're born selfish. From the time you first learned to walk and talk, it was all about you. It was all about mine, mine, mine. That's okay because we're all human. However, as an adult, if you wake up each day, thinking only about the person you see in the mirror, you'll soon be left with only that same person in the mirror in your life. I've been there, and, maybe you've been there as well. It's cool for a while, but soon the lunch, dinner, movie, and/or chips on the sofa, "Party of One" gets really old, really fast.

Here's where the work comes in: The difference between selfishness and selflessness is often the gap preventing two sides of any type of relationship, romantic, business, or otherwise from prospering.

The mental OneMoreStep worth taking is to make a conscious effort to let go of the "my tendencies," obsessing over my time, my money, my stuff, and/or my career. It's simple, but not necessarily easy, because it rarely happens automatically.

In fact, leading with a Compro-My's attitude is unnatural. That's where the work comes into play for you and me both. It's a choice available to you in every single situation. Either you want to put in the effort necessary to make the relationship work, or you don't.

When you choose to do the work, to Compro-My's; your relationships change for the better; in most cases, for good. Something also happens to that person you look at every morning in the mirror; they also change for good.

All it takes is a little effort. That conscientious effort is waiting for you, in the gap between selfishness and selflessness. Fill in this all too familiar gap with compassion and compromise. In a sea of sameness in corporate America, you'll stand out as a person who'll listen, share, care, and as the one willing to do the hard work essential to connect and collaborate. You'll be known as one who cares more about the team's or the organization's accomplishments than your own personal achievements.

That's leadership. That's teamwork. That's serving.

What does Compro-My's look like in the corporate setting?

- Offering to pick up your peer's Saturday night shift so she can attend her daughter's basketball game
- Arriving early or staying late, without being asked – giving your own time, and *giving* of yourself to the team, your boss, or best of all, your Guests, customers, and clients
- Pausing, staying quiet, and remaining calm when someone shares a *not-so-intelligent* idea or worse, when someone disagrees with your idea. After the pause, offer to try it their way for a while, in the spirit of compromise.
- Recognizing the passion, commitment, and dedication of the folks on the team before taking credit yourself, even when you know you've kinda crushed it in your own right. Remember – you never look bad making somebody else look good.

Show me a person willing to compromise, with compassion for people, "making the extra pass" and I'll show you a person who can connect and foster relationships with anyone, anytime. Show me a person with that level of relationship-ability, and I'll show you a person who can inspire, motivate, and drive a team forward.

That's the person I want on my team, that's the person I want as my own leader, and that's the person I want to be at work and at home.

Don't you?

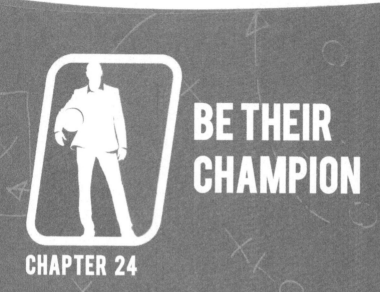

BE THEIR CHAMPION

CHAPTER 24

Whether you love your current job or hate it, you probably work alongside, with, or for people you may or may not like. Some are cool, but others are not cool at all. Let's be honest. Some people just, well, never mind. We'll keep it positive, here, but you know what I mean.

Be "That" Person You Know and Love

Usually, in every job or situation there's a person who has a way of making it all better. Do you know them? Maybe you have one or two in your life, and you're thinking about them now. They're the people who make a rainy day seem bright and sunny, an aggravating project fun, and they can even make a boring email hilarious. They're simply the best part of your day.

Consider with me for a second the coach, teacher, leader, parent, friend, coworker, or family member who instantly comes to mind. You know, that person in your life who is:

- Encouraging, and your biggest cheerleader no matter what
- Accepting of your weirdness because they see it as unique and special
- Rooting for you even when others root against you
- Forgiving every time you mess up and fall short
- Friends with everyone; not because they have to, but because they want to
- Inspiring with their unconditional love and compassion toward anyone in their midst

What would you do without them? For starters, you'd feel less encouraged, less forgiven, less inspired, and you'd probably have one or two fewer people to call true friends, confidantes or advocates. Whoever they are, and whether it's at home or at work, we love that person in our lives. We light up when we see them in the office. Sometimes just a quick glimpse, email, instant message, or a text from them calms our nerves, chills us out, and makes us smile.

They're such a blessing. Work would suck without them.

As awesome as they are, who says we can't also be *that person* for others?

It's time. We can. I can. You can. With compassion and compromise at the forefront of our hearts and minds, *that person* we'll absolutely be.

Sure, when others look up to you or turn to you, always watching and listening to what you say or when people begin doing what you've encouraged them to do, the responsibility on your shoulders can be daunting. But that's leadership. Remember it's "accepting the challenge to influence" which makes leaders, leaders.

You can do it. It all starts with compassion and having an attitude of an advocate. Want to be a game-changer? Want to really step up, influence, improve, inspire, and change lives? For your own life, do you want less frustration, hurt, despair, and depression? Me, too.

Have an Attitude of an Advocate

Compassion is the answer. This attitude of an advocate is even more than an attitude; it's an overwhelming spirit. When you decide to be *that person* to others, you'll be changed for good. You won't be able to shake it and you'll become the leader you never knew you could be. How will you feel it? How will you know you're leading? After weeks and weeks and months and months of *conversation after conversation*, you'll turn around and see a line of people following you. They'll lean into your leadership, coaching, and direction because you'll have proven just how much you care about them and their future.

This spirit and attitude is one of compassion, grace, mercy and love. If you've ever been encouraged or inspired, touched, motivated, or personally changed by someone, you know how unbelievable it feels. If you haven't, that's okay, because guess what? When you become *that person* for people in the office, at the gym, at your "dumb job" or especially at home, and when you're the encourager, inspirer, forgiver, and motivator, you'll feel it. You'll feel the overwhelming spirit, and it will be so, so good. Your heart will be so full of grace and love that your mind will forget all about the frustrating, demoralizing *corporate corporateness* you deal with daily at work.

Look for the Good in People

Every summer of my college years, I interned on the Walt Disney World College Program, in Orlando, FL. Each summer I worked in a different line of business in a totally new and different location. The summer before my senior year, I worked at Disney's All Star Movies Resort, as a Merchandise Sales Host. My shift was the highly sought-after, 5:00 pm to 1:30 am swing shift.

Brutal.

I remember calling my Mom a couple weeks into the summer, whining and complaining, "It's awful, Mom! The hours are stupid, I never get to see any of my friends, and the people at work are all older! Much older." I was a bit spoiled because the summer prior I worked at Disney's Animal Kingdom Theme Park, as an Attractions Host at *It's Tough to Be a Bug*. I loved that summer because I got to work with twenty or thirty other college age students also interning for the summer. We worked together, played together, and may or may not have partied together. To say it was fun is an understatement.

Now, I was dropped in the middle of the swing shift with people my parents' age, working until the wee hours of the morning in an off-the-beaten path resort (albeit a Disney Resort, but I was spoiled.). Poor me.

My mom challenged me to find something fun and interesting about every one of those people at *Donald's Double Feature* merchandise shop at Disney's All-Star Movies Resort. I took her advice the very next day (*or night*) at work.

It worked!

As soon as I got over my self-pity, and started engaging with my fellow Cast Members and even my leaders, the summer changed. In fact, my life may have changed. The more I stepped out of my shell and into the opportunity to engage with and learn from the people with whom I worked despite their age, the more interesting and fun work became. Imagine that. All it took was being a bit more interested in other people:

- How I could help them,
- What I could learn from them, and
- How much fun they really could be.

By the end of that summer, my leaders approached me about my future with Disney. I was entering my senior year of undergrad, and they told me they were putting my name into a candidate pool for management interns to be selected for the following summer. I was flattered, and of course eagerly accepted the endorsement. They probably never would've championed me for the Leadership Candidate Pool had I not changed my tune earlier in the summer.

Throughout my nearly twenty years working in corporate America, I could always lean on a call to my mom on my commute home with tales for her about this person or that one, this stupid thing or that one. I spoke to her with enough frustration, angst, and bitterness to float a battleship, but Mom had a simple suggestion every time.

It would go something like this, "Well, it sounds like someone is getting a little too consumed with himself. But that's okay. It's time for you to go focus on making someone else's day. Try focusing on doing something for somebody other than yourself. You'll feel much better."

That suggestion, along with countless other lessons from Mom, have always had a 100 percent success rate. If success, in this context, is defined as squashing my own frustrations, bitterness, and rage against all the "slackers" and "jerks" at work, then, yep, it's literally undefeated.

There's no other answer or antidote. This "Mom Tip" works like a charm, 100 percent of the time. Deciding to simply *be that person* for other people keeps you grounded. Even though you're hustling, staying around the ball, earning it, doing vs. trying, and crushing it in your own right, compassion keeps a nice balance of your focus on others during your own growing success.

Crushing it and "playing like a champion" is one thing. However, championing others and encouraging your teammates, friends, family or mentees to crush it is next level stuff. That's where game-change resides, for you and for them. Give it a try. Make an effort to champion other people.

Thoughts on Champions

Champions are special.

They're usually "the best," the "winners" and deserving of the title. They're talented, skillful, and have earned everyone's respect.

They didn't get there alone. Often, champions had a coach, a mentor, a leader, supporters, advocates, and they had champions encouraging them along the way.

Look up the word champion; (champ · pi · on) – on Merriam-Webster.com and the number one noun definition reads, "Warrior, fighter".

One verb definition reads, "To act as militant supporter of..." Oooh, I like that one, too.

Champions become so special because of all the championing they got along the way. Think how awesome you would be if you literally had warriors and fighters, actively and uncompromisingly supporting you.

Better yet, how awesome would you and I be, if we were the ones championing? What if we were the coaches, mentors, leaders, supporters, and advocates who ultimately inspired that special someone at work to go OneMoreStep, reach for the stars, diligently dream their dreams, realize their full potential, and/or help them become the person God created them to be?

Champions and advocates are special. Be that person to champion others, with an attitude of an advocate. Your heart will be so full of grace and gratefulness it literally won't have room left for frustration, depression, or bitterness.

Be that person to champion others, with an attitude of an advocate.

By the way, if you think you don't have *that person* in your life. You do. Look up. He's right there, championing you, as your advocate, loving you more than you will ever fathom. God is your ultimate champion. He's mine too. It feels great – it feels encouraging, inspiring, forgiving, and accepting. That's what it's all about.

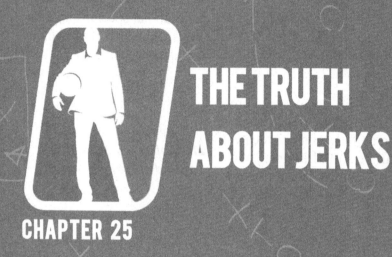

THE TRUTH ABOUT JERKS

CHAPTER 25

I know what you're probably thinking. I'm thinking the same thing; some people can be total jerks. How in the world could I possibly be *that person* to *champion* these total and complete jerks in my life?

Some Thoughts on Jerks

People sometimes act like jerks. No question, it's an unfortunate reality. The fortunate reality is or can be, about how you choose to react when people around you act like a jerk.

They may NOT know better.

Though it may be hard to believe, the person on the other end of the phone, across the aisle, across the conference room table, or in the next room, may not know how to act or react in certain situations. In some cases, even if they know what's right, they may not know how to show it, say it or do it.

Something else may be happening right now in his or her life because everyone has stuff. Any of these sound familiar?

- The student whose bad attitude compromises the teacher/student connection
- The VP, Director, or boss who's always in a hurry and rarely listens
- Our friend who always seems down in the dumps, sad and in a bad mood
- The client who gives you a hard time and wants it his way or the highway
- The person on our team who quacks and gripes about everything

They snap at us, they cut people off mid-sentence and they don't engage. On the surface, they're a total jerk face. It's easy to ignore them, distance yourself from them, and sometimes even snap back at them.

In these instances, tell yourself that everyone has "stuff." Be the one person who takes five minutes out of your day to show them you care and you also want to help.

Maybe they're upset about a speeding ticket they got on the way to work. They may have just had a fight with their significant other. Or worse, maybe they just broke up with their girlfriend or boyfriend. Maybe they're going through a messy divorce.

That student or coworker with the bad attitude, what if he or she has a learning disability, which makes it difficult to focus in class or at work? That rude coworker or staff member may be worried to death about a sick family member, or their own health. The truth is - we never know. Think how much stress you have in your life. You're not alone. Everybody has "stuff."

Jerks aren't native to our current location or place of employment.

We have a natural tendency to overly romanticize "the next season" or "our next place of employment." You know, the ideal place or perfect company where everything will be so much better. Truth is, the grass isn't greener with fewer "jerks" onboard someplace else. Jerks have a funny way of surfacing, no matter where we find ourselves.

They're Probably Scared of Something

One of my favorite authors and guru on leadership and marketing, Seth Godin, published a blog post several years ago entitled, "Snark and Fear." The main idea was if and when people get snarky with us; we should ask, "What are you afraid of?" Chances are, when people get snippy, testy, or short with others or us, it's rooted in fear. In corporate settings, they're either afraid of losing money or even losing their job. They also may be insecure and might fear losing their reputation, status, or credibility with certain audiences; usually the big wigs.

Jerks Have Needs Sometimes

They might need help. Whether it's financial assistance, someone they can call a friend, someone to make them laugh, or perhaps just something or someone to put their mind at ease, they may have a huge hole the size of Texas in their life, and they need something or someone.

Once I had to coach a very high performer on my team. She was incredibly frustrated and came into my office unleashing a full six minutes of complete and utter negativity. I'm not even sure she came up for air during her rant. She said a few things earlier in the day too, and, I intended to have a conversation with her before the end of the day. I took the opportunity the moment she was in my office rattling off endless complaint after complaint, some of which were even directed toward me.

As she finally caught her breath in-between complaints, I took it as my opportunity to coach. I leaned into what I knew could be a wonderful, teachable moment to inspire her. She rolled her eyes and stormed out of my office as I was speaking to her.

I was like, wait…what?! Did that just happen?

I made sure my message was delivered to her before she left for the day. I talked to her candidly, openly and honestly. Suffice it to say, I set clear expectations and accountability measures on respect and courtesy, especially in the context of communicating with her leaders.

A couple weeks later once tempers had calmed, she was in my office again. This time her mood was positive. I brought up the events of that not-so-magical day. While she understood why I coached her that day, she finally opened up. She told me earlier in that not-so-magical-day someone else was a jerk and popped off with insensitive, hurtful words toward her. As she was telling me this, her voice began to crack and tears welled up behind her eyes. She was visibly hurting.

She'd been working incredibly hard, staying late, coming in early, and consistently leading her peers and even her own leaders, me included. She didn't deserve those tactless comments. When she came into my office that afternoon, she needed to vent. She told me she just needed someone to listen. She didn't need me to fix anything. She needed a shoulder, and I was doing the opposite of what she needed in that moment.

I had been impressed with her since the day we met. She was smart, charismatic, fun and had an unbelievable work ethic. She just had an edge, one all too similar to my own. Most of the time her edge was a good thing, but her irritable and easily frustrated state reminded me of my own. I wanted to help her, and teach her how pride, frustration, and a short fuse could get her in trouble one day as that attitude once got me fired earlier in my career.

Her vulnerability and openness, telling me all she needed was a shoulder in that moment was probably the most impressed I'd felt toward her up until that point. Why? It was her authenticity, finally opening up, genuinely sharing her feelings. She wasn't being a jerk a couple weeks earlier. She felt hurt and needed something. She needed me to be there for her. And I simply wasn't. I failed her as a leader, as a partner, and as her champion.

Wait. Maybe, in reality jerks aren't jerks after all.

It could be they might not be as bad as we think.

Not sold? Still not buying it?

I wasn't either until I remembered I've been a jerk toward people at one time or another. Then I thought, "Wouldn't it be nice if people gave me the benefit of the doubt when I have an 'off day' and act like a total jerk?"

That's reason enough to be more compassionate to the "jerks" in our lives. Because honestly, they're no different than us. I bet deep down, they're not jerks at all.

So, when people act like total jerks, smile right back at them. Meet them where they are, and perhaps even figure out a way to help them. It could be the difference that matters. For every jerk or jerky comment there's an opportunity to love someone through it, with compassion in your heart.

So, when people act like total jerks, smile right back at them.

Too often we try to get back at them, win the argument, or prove our point. Every time I do that I get in trouble or make matters worse. Then, who's the jerk?

That's the truth about jerks.

Resentment and Change

Since jerks may not know better, or they have something else going on in their life, or they're a little scared of something, or they're currently in desperate need of something, you can find it a little easier to respond with compassion.

Don't resent them just yet. Fight the urge to resent, detest, and hate them right away. They could be grappling with a huge ordeal, and their words, actions, and overall jerkiness may not be completely because of you or even aimed toward you.

Perhaps more importantly, guard against changing because of what they've said about you. It's easy to fall into it, but it's another trap. You know the feeling. When *they* say or do things to put you down, demean you, or prop themselves up, it's natural to feel like you need to change.

Um, no.

They're acting like a jerk. They're not the end all be all. They're not the all-knowing authority on the world or your life. It sounds simple enough, but we've all been there, with people disparaging us and hating on us. Our first reaction is to change something – our stance, our approach, or even our beliefs or values. Absolutely not.

Believe you belong just as you are. Believe in your values and character, even in these moments - in fact, especially in these moments. Don't change simply because some jerk says you should. They're hurting or afraid of something. This may be their way of working through their hurt or pain. Coach Baker sent me a text one morning while I was writing this book. It was a picture of a banner hanging in his school gymnasium with quote that read,

"Don't let your character change color with your environment. Find out who you are and let it stay its true color."

~ Rachel Joy Scott

Remember to reveal your own character despite others revealing their less than stellar character. Here's another truth, compassion to this extent doesn't always come naturally. The only way to drum up the compassion to think about, accept, and even help jerks is to open up and love them. More on love in the next chapter. See you there.

AFASTPASS THROUGH CORPORATE CORPORATENESS

CHAPTER 26

Friday September 16th, 2016 was the most special and incredible day of my life. It was the day my wife, Jenna, and I were married. We wanted our wedding to be a blend of traditional and nontraditional, as our relationship is a smidge unconventional, to say the least.

We met while both of us were on vacation at Walt Disney World, in Orlando, FL in early November of 2011. She lived in Seattle and I lived in Las Vegas. After a one-year long distance relationship, she moved to Las Vegas. That was the best sale I've ever closed, convincing a Pacific Northwest girl to move to the desert.

Love Can

Back to our wedding day…

One of the subtle, unconventional twists in our wedding was rather than Jenna walking down the aisle to the traditional, "Here Comes the

Bride" processional; she walked down the aisle to a song entitled, "Love Can." It not only represented our journey together up to that point, but also the very foundation on which we are building our marriage. The foundation I'm referring to is love - specifically, the love of God.

The song was written by Drew Bodine, lead musical pastor at Central Christian Church, which was my church in Las Vegas for several years. When Jenna moved to Vegas, of course it became *our church*. In September of 2013, Central embarked on a mission to take its ministry and reach new heights. The tag line for our journey was simply, LOVE CAN.

It was our thankful response of gratitude to what God's love had done for us, and our faithful response for what we believed God's love would do to further the ministry. On September 29th, 2013, Central held a church service dubbed, "Pack the Mack", at the Thomas & Mack Center near the campus of UNLV. Over 15,000 people from all over the Vegas valley literally packed the Thomas & Mack Center, moved to worship, smack dab in the middle of Las Vegas less than a mile away from the legendary Strip. This was proof if God can show up in this way, in "Sin City," chances are He can show up wherever you find yourself, literally and figuratively.

The underlying concept of Love Can is there are so many things we want to do for ourselves, for others, and maybe even for God. Some things, while we want them, dream about them, and feel passionately about them, are just too far out of reach. We kind of realize, deep down, though we want it, we're not sure we'll ever achieve it. We say, "I could never really do that." We don't even know where to start.

Exactly. You can't. I can't. But God's love can.

Enter Love Can.

God's love can do things we cannot. God's love is more powerful, deeper, more meaningful, and far-reaching. We couldn't possibly fathom the things He can do. He can heal the sick, feed the poor, move mountains, part seas, and make miracles happen; you know, all the highlights from Sunday School. He can also do things like:

- Give us strength when we need it,
- Patience when we're so over it,

- Peace when things seem to be falling apart,
- Hope when we're hopeless, and
- Comfort when we're freaking out,
- Clarity when we're confused, and
- Direction when we don't even know where to start.

Jenna and I fell in love somewhere between the fall of 2011 and the spring of 2012. We'd talk on the phone, FaceTime, text, Facebook, Instagram, and email daily. Okay, more like hourly. After work, hitting the gym, and protein shakes, we'd FaceTime each other and fantasize about what our future might look like together. Would we live in Seattle? Vegas? Orlando? Neither of us had a clue. We just knew we wanted to be together somewhere. One night, we decided a great dream compromise would be California. We jokingly fantasized about becoming "a coastal couple." Mind you, at the time I lived in the desert and she lived in the Pacific Northwest. But hey, a dream is a wish your heart makes, right?

Neither of us knew how to make it happen. It seemed like a pipe dream. So many things would have to happen, at the right time, and both of us would need to be in the right mindset. Speaking of Vegas, the odds were literally stacked against us.

Yet here I sit today, writing this chapter in beautiful Southern California, which is where we live. We don't live in a mansion, though there are many around us. We don't have the nicest home, nor do we even own it. Our apartment is nestled along a golf course with views of the Pacific Ocean. After fantasizing about it just four years prior, with no clue how or if it could or would happen, here we are.

We became that coastal couple we always dreamed of becoming. It didn't "just happen." Love made it happen: God's love, our love for God first, and for each other, second. We loved each other enough to take some risks. Though risky, we put our faith in God, and we've always made our relationship about Him first and each other second.

What does my love life, my wedding, and our dreams of living on the coast in California have to do with *Ballgames to Boardrooms*? Not sure.

Kidding!

It's all about love - specifically, the unfathomable, unbelievable, and unconditional love of God. Jenna and I started off in a long-distance relationship between Seattle and Las Vegas, with no clue how on Earth we'd somehow end up in the same city, let alone married. Then, on top of that, we've since been able to live our "California coastal couple" pipe dream.

On the surface, it all seemed flat out impossible. Yet, with faith in and through God's love and love for each other, our journey in retrospect was quite possible. Why? Because love can do things mere mortals simply cannot do without it.

Love can.

Your Secret Weapon to Fight the Corporate Fight

This truth is transferable to the corporate grind when all too often the tasks, initiatives, people, bosses, and the deliverables are nothing less than impossible. When incorporating all the strategies and tactics on the pages of Ballgames to Boardrooms sounds like an overwhelming task. Not so fast. Remember to *lead with love*, your secret weapon.

Remember to lead with love, your secret weapon.

Leaders and future leaders who lead with love as opposed to leading through fear or intimidation, not only have stronger, more successful teams, they also achieve more meaning, fulfillment, and happiness along their journey. I've tried it both ways. Maybe you've tried it a few different ways and you've experienced a few different styles of your own leaders and coaches along the way.

Love is the only way. In the throes of corporate America including the pressure, the numbers, the initiatives, the group work on steroids, the dissension, the gossip, the blaming, finger-pointing, victimizing, posturing, grandstanding, and the occasional good day which keeps you going back the next – love is our only hope.

Love in Action

What does *leading with love* look like? Simply look to 1 Corinthians to see the way:

- **"Love is patient."** When the people in your life don't get it on the first, second, or even third attempt, be patient. When your own boss is less than patient, and/or keeps changing the task, objective, or direction, be patient. When your team or certain individuals are less than professional, less astute, or when they're "Needy Neidersons," be patient. *That's leading with love.*

- **"Love is kind."** It will get stupid. The deadlines, expectations, timing or lack thereof, the workloads, and even the people will be difficult. Two quotes sum up this principle. Plato said, "Be kind. Everyone is fighting a tough, inner battle you know nothing about."

  Tim McGraw said, "Always stay humble and kind. Hold the door, say please, say thank you; don't steal, don't cheat, and don't lie. I know ya got mountains to climb, but always stay humble and kind." *That's leading with love.*

- **"Love does not envy."** Your friends will get promoted and make a lot of money. Your boss will likely always make more money than you. Some of your peers, and maybe even the people you lead will make more money than you. They'll own bigger houses, take more lavish vacations, and probably drive nicer cars. Don't be jealous of what they have, or what you don't have. Be thankful for what you do have. It could always be worse. Congratulate them on their success, and keep crushing life, doing your very best, today. Tomorrow will take care of itself. Today is the day. *That's leading with love.*

- **"Love does not boast."** When you crush it, get the promotion, the raise, nail it on the project, deliver a dime speech or presentation, move mountains of executive bureaucratic corporate corporateness, and when you receive accolades, acknowledgments, or high praise, (*and I know you will*) don't brag. Put your head down, and circle the bases. Act like you've been there before. Then, go right back to serving other people. *That's leading with love.*

- **"Love is not proud."** Remember a temporary flare up of pride can potentially cause pain forever, for you, for them, and for your career. Know when those two culprits, pride and ego, are beginning to rise and bubble up to the surface. Tell yourself, "It's not worth it to make this point to win the conversation." Just *breathe in, breathe out, and move on*, like the Jimmy Buffett song. *That's leading with love.*

- **"Love does not dishonor others."** When others get engrossed in gossip, putting down the boss, the slackers, the mean girls, the mean boys, and the unfortunate shortcomings of the job, company, or even the task at hand, keep it positive. Like my grandfather PopPop used to tell me, "If you don't have anything nice to say, don't say anything at all." *That's leading with love.*

- **"Love is not self-seeking."** Make it about *them*. In a society and in a corporate America full of self-serving leaders, become a servant leader. Remember, you never look bad making someone else look good. Make the extra pass. *That's leading with love.*

- **"Love is not easily angered."** Live and work for an audience of one. If the boss, her boss, or his boss says something rude, crude, or downright despicable, rise above it. It doesn't matter what they think anyway. The only thing that matters is what God thinks. To quote former First Lady Michelle Obama, "When they go low, you go high." Remember to be slow to speak, quick to listen, and slow to anger (James 1:19). *That's leading with love.*

- **"Love always protects, always trusts, always hopes, and always perseveres."** Protect the people on your team. Coach them when they need it, saving them from making more mistakes. Trust them before you know you can. Don't let them give up hope. In fact, be the hope in their lives, and don't ever stop believing in, standing up for, and doing the right thing. *That's leading with love.*

The Irony of Self Help

The irony of writing or reading "self-help" books is funny. Millions of people before us and millions who'll come after us will try to do it on their own. You and I do, too. As we've discussed in earlier chapters, we tend to be control freaks. It's okay because we come by it naturally. We were born that way. Remember? "Mine, mine, mine…" was our refrain when we were children.

We can't do this alone. The special ingredient that makes the impossible, possible is love. The fast pass of all fast passes which turns the doldrums of corporate corporateness into meaningful work is love. The one and only answer and antidote to anger, jealousy, disappointment, frustration, loneliness, hurts, habits, and hang ups, of your own or of those you lead is love.

After nearly twenty years of starts, stops, new jobs, new industries, new cities, new relationships, great leaders, terrible leaders, and mediocre leaders, I can honestly tell you *leading with love* is not only a better way; it's the only way. Love is the only way to make your team happy, your boss happy, and to simply be happy. Unless or until you're happy, you'll always be left with a significant void in your life.

You want to be happy. I want you to be happy. And, I kind of want to be happy too. Lead with love, in everything you do, and happiness will have a funny way of popping up in your day-to-day grind.

"Darkness cannot drive out darkness; only light can do that. Hate cannot drive out hate; only love can do that."

~ Martin Luther King, Jr.

GIFTS FROM A COACH

CONCLUSION

As I'm sure you've noticed, my childhood and high school years were largely centered on the game of basketball - watching, playing, coaching, learning, practicing, or dreaming about basketball. I loved it then and I still love it. I always looked up to my coaches and I still do.

When I was a senior, Coach Baker brought a gift to our house. It was a beautifully framed, still life print, filled with authentic memorabilia representing "Kentucky Life." The print featured an array of memorabilia unique to Kentucky and Bluegrass Life.

Earlier in that school year, I saw this print in his office, and commented on how cool it was. Months later Coach gave it to me as a graduation gift. If that's not proof Coach walks his talk and practices what he preaches about listening, I don't know what is. I was impressed he paid such close attention and remembered my comment about the print in his office a few months before. He was truly listening, and never missed a beat.

My grandfather went to all my high school (and Junior High, for that matter) basketball games, sat in the front row, and cheered us on, win or lose. We always knew he was there, rockin' his navy-blue winter hat regardless of the temperature outdoors or inside the gymnasium. During sophomore year at Florida Southern College, my grandfather, Nick DeSantis, who we loved as PopPop, went home to Heaven. I flew back to Kentucky for the funeral of course to be with my family.

In addition to visiting with family, Coach Baker sent a special gift, addressed to me. It was an ordinary-looking, white, wooden clock, but the message Coach sent was extraordinary. He knew about my close relationship with PopPop. He also knew how tough this life event would be for me. The card simply read, *"It just takes time..."* He later explained in person, how accepting losing PopPop would get easier with time. Also, to hang in there, staying strong for my mom, aunt, uncle, and grandmother.

When I saw Coach at the funeral home, he came up to me, gave me a bear hug, and told me how PopPop was a loyal East Carter Raider basketball fan long before I came along. We shared some laughs with several folks gathered around, told stories about PopPop, and he stayed, visiting with family for hours during that tough time.

Since leaving my hometown to pursue my education and business career, I've lived in Lakeland, FL, Orlando, FL, Ithaca, NY, Las Vegas, NV, Miami, FL, Orlando, FL (again), and then Las Vegas, NV (again), and Southern California. The *"Kentucky Legacy"* print and the white clock are both proudly displayed in my home today. I've kept them on display, with every move I've made over the years.

I share this story because it's a great metaphor for both the opportunity and gift of *COACHING*. The clock and beautiful *Kentucky Legacy* print were tangible *gifts*. My parents, along with Coach Charles Baker, Coach Hager Easterling, Coach Doc Bender, and Coach Jack Calhoun Jr., during my high school years, also gave me countless *intangible gifts*, as they taught, illustrated, encouraged, and pushed me, almost daily; to strive for excellence. *They coached, in every sense of the word.* The *gifts* of their coaching all those years ago are still relevant in my life, and they guide me in business every day. Can you relate? I'm sure your own coaches shared with you many *gifts*, lessons, and encouragement earlier in your life as well.

Lean into Incredible Opportunities

For leaders, bosses, teachers, professors, doctors, lawyers, or actual *coaches* of teams, never underestimate the opportunity you have, to *teach* and *coach*. No matter what your rank, role, or title, you never know how impactful and meaningful your words may be to the people on your teams and in your life.

If you're a leader or a leader among your peers on the brink of breaking through to management or even the executive ranks (and something tells me you're closer than you think), you can bet they're watching. They're watching you, listening to you, and following you. You're leading in more ways than you think. You're capable. You're passionate. You're compassionate. You love them, so coach them.

Lean into it. Step up, and lean into the opportunity to teach, coach, encourage, advocate, support, and deliver your message. You have the understanding, the talent, the vision, the work ethic, and the attitude of an advocate. You've earned the right to be a coach. So, go ahead and coach.

Step One – Give. Step Two – Repeat Step One.

Before writing this book, a few people asked, "What do you want readers of your book to be able to do after they read it?"

The short answer is I want you and everyone who reads Ballgames to Boardrooms to generate a few new ideas or maybe even a few action plans for making your work life or personal life more fun, meaningful, significant, and happy. However, I personally care less about what this book inspires you to do. It's more about what these 26 chapters inspire you to *give*.

After all, I dug deep to write these chapters, from the bottom of my heart and soul because several people - my parents, coaches, teachers, professors, leaders, and peers first *gave* me the gifts of their coaching. The reality is, we're all able to get up and do the "fill-in-the-blank thing" – whether it's work, play, or otherwise - because someone first *gave us* something. Someone first gave you a lesson, an education, a pearl of wisdom, an idea, or an opportunity, and then you were able to "do."

Go be that someone for someone else. They're waiting for your gifts.

At the beginning of our conversation and the beginning of this book, you thought back to when you were younger, playing sports. We all played sports to have fun, belong to a team, put our talents to good use, and experience fulfillment, before we even knew what *fulfillment* meant. For leaders, be it coaching a sports team or a team in corporate America, encouraging your teams to *practice, work hard, listen to coaches, have fun,* and *unleash compassion* will absolutely lead them to a happier, more fulfilling, more meaningful life – both at work and at home. Those same principles by which you lead will result in a happier, more fulfilling, and more meaningful life for you as well.

Corporate America takes and takes and takes. Bosses, Managers, and corporations take all the time, work, energy, value, ingenuity, and mental capacity they possibly can from us. Coaches, true leaders, on the other hand, *give.* They give gifts. They teach lessons and build people up rather than breaking them down. Coaches listen, they love, and they foster relationships with and among their teams. Coaches make an indelible mark on the very lives and people they touch with their grace, mercy, compassion, and love.

Go. Change Lives Forever, Including Your Own

Whether you're a leader in sports, corporate America, or in your community, never underestimate the *gifts from a coach.* Never underestimate the gifts you've been given, or the ones you'll gift to your friends, family, team, and organization. If delivered appropriately, the gifts of your coaching will last forever. They'll be passed on to person after person, team after team, and generation after generation.

I hope you give your gifts to everyone and anyone willing to receive them. You'll change lives for the better. Heaven knows the gifts from my coaches over the years have and continue to change my life. I'm sure you feel the same way about your own coaches.

This book is my way of giving you the gifts I've received from coaches. If you like them, use them. If you use them, and they work for you and others, share them. People are waiting for gifts from a coach, and you can be the coach who changes someone's life.

So, practice the future today. *"Play" (work) hard, listen to your own coaches, have fun,* and *unleash compassion.* You'll transform your boring job into meaningful work, achieve fulfillment, inevitable success, and most importantly, you'll enjoy the ride.

ACKNOWLEDGEMENTS

This is my first book, and the process of bringing it to life started long before I put pen to paper. Like anything in sports, business, or life, it takes a team for any project to go from inception to completion. I certainly had help in writing this book, and I'd like to acknowledge the people who helped me bring it to life:

To the best coaches ever, my parents, Mary Cass and Jeffrey Scott, thank you for teaching me and coaching me life lessons, on and off the court, inside and outside the classroom, and most importantly, at home at the kitchen table. Everything I have today, and everywhere I've been or will ever go is because of the love, support, and encouragement you've given me all my life. I love you.

To my wife, Jenna, thank you for not only entertaining me every single day, brining an abundance of joy, laughter, and love into my life, but also entertaining my often outlandish ideas and dreams for our current and future adventures. You inspire me everyday, and I love you.

To Coach Charles Baker, you've been "Coach" to me, my entire life. I've looked up to you, listened, observed, and hung on your every lesson and our every conversation since I was a five-year old boy with big dreams – basketball and otherwise. Thank you for the many lessons on the court, which have proven transferable to countless situations off the court. I love basketball and still eat, sleep, and breathe MTXE to this day. I love you.

To all my other basketball coaches, Coach Hager Easterling, Coach Tim Kennedy, Coach Jack Calhoun Jr., Coach Doc Bender, Coach Donald Damron, Coach Barrett Bush, Coach Brandon Baker, my college basketball coach, Coach Gordon Gibbons, my Little League

Baseball coach, Tim Baldwin, and to my YMCA league soccer coach, the late Bill Ticknor, thank you for putting up with my bundle of nerves back then, and teaching me to harness my passion. I remain a work in progress to harness that same passion as an adult. Your words of wisdom and coaching ring as loud and clear in my head today as they did all those years ago on the court and on the field. I haven't forgotten, and I love all of you.

To Tom McMahon, my boss during the Wynn|Encore Las Vegas season of my career; thanks for taking a chance on a 28-year old. I didn't know what I was doing, and I was scared. Your lessons, teachings, and conversations with me during my year with you not only got me through each trying day, but have also helped me execute and add value in every job since. I'm not sure I ever really properly thanked you. I love you.

To Colleen Birch, my boss during the Cosmopolitan of Las Vegas season of my career, thank you for believing in me and trusting me. You trusted me to lead with love, passion, and compassion, and that is simply rare and different, in today's corporate America. I was often frustrated, but you always listened and loved me through the peaks and valleys. I love you.

To Brian Gress, my mentor and friend during that same Cosmopolitan of Las Vegas season. I learned more from you than you know. Corporate Corporateness is a "thing", and you helped me get better at some intangible things I never knew I needed to improve; several of those lessons were just shared in these pages. I am grateful for you, and I love you.

To Ken Potrock, Sr. VP and General Manager of Disney Vacation Club, Adventures by Disney, and Golden Oak at Walt Disney World, thank you for taking a chance on me. You believed in me despite my unconventional resume and unconventional style of leadership. Thank you for always making me feel valued and for being ok with me writing this book in my time away from work at DVC.

To Mark Sanborn, NY Times best-selling author and hall of fame speaker, thank you for answering a Facebook message from me in 2011. You're my favorite author. You not only introduced me to Fred the Postman, but you also taught me how to deliver breakthrough speeches.   You always inspire me to turn the ordinary into the extraordinary. I value and appreciate our relationship. I love you.

To my book coach, Denise Michaels, who piqued my interest with a LinkedIn article on *reasons not to write a book*! I didn't even know book coaching was a "thing", but I'm glad it is, because your coaching, encouragement, and partnership have been lessons I truly never knew I needed in order to write a book. Thank you, and I love you.

To Lin-Manuel Miranda, whose own personal story, the story of Alexander Hamilton, the music, and lyrics of *Hamilton – An American Musical*, inspired me to *write my way out, non-stop* at coffee shops, on airplanes, on my couch, at my kitchen table, and even in the shower. Your music, stories, and lyrics moved me to move others. If it took this project and/or this acknowledgment for us to meet, it will have been worth it. If you don't know, now you know.

To THE Coach of all coaches, God, you're the only audience that matters. This book is ultimately for you because of you, and if it enhances even one person's relationship with you then writing it will have absolutely, positively been worth it!

Ballgame.

Bring Taylor Scott to Your Organization, Meeting, or Event

Since 2010, Taylor has engaged audiences in Colleges and Universities, Community Organizations, School Districts, and Fortune 500 companies.

His entertaining and inspirational messages leave audiences with actionable strategies on HOW TO:

- Inspire connection among Teams, Guests, and Customers (Increase Engagement)
- Develop and become better leaders (Increasing Profitability)
- Transform menial jobs into meaningful work (Increasing Productivity)
- Encourage, Coach, and Motivate (Close the Millennial / Gen X / Baby Boomer Gap)

Book Taylor as a speaker for your event at www.BallgamesToBoardrooms.com/speak